Government Deals Are Funded, Not Sold

As identified by Bloomberg Government, the best-performing federal contractors all lobby Congress. We might guess that intuitively. The common perception of Washington, DC, as an insider's game, persists, and it makes sense that the winners lobby. However, focusing only on best-performing contractors limits the view of what unfolds through congressional lobbying or, more importantly, could unfold for even more companies—if they only recognized that they also have access to Congress. The tools of congressional influence are available to every company, yet the overwhelming majority of federal contractors eschew the opportunity to lobby Congress. Sadly, it's not just that companies often don't know how. It's worse; *they don't know why lobbying Congress can be helpful.*

Defense represents the most significant portion of the federal budget annually reviewed and approved by Congress. As such, it's a valuable case study to understand what may contribute to a concentration of winners that garner federal contracts. Any company can learn by understanding more about lobbying in the defense industry.

The inability or unwillingness to integrate lobbying into a sales strategy stems from hubris, ignorance, and lack of imagination. Thinking, "I've got this," and relying on their wits and narrow networks, too many defense executives struggle to gain real traction and consistently win large contracts. The result? The biggest winners aggregate at the top of the defense industrial base pyramid, while the hundreds of thousands of "others" are left to wonder what just happened and why it's so hard.

This book focuses on those who do not lobby. It's almost too easy to conclude that the system is unfair, unlikely to change, and populated by well-connected insiders who move through the revolving door. Digging a little deeper, this book reveals that the real challenge to more democratized access to Congress is within our reach—if we could only see it!

Government Deals Are Funded, Not Sold

How to Incorporate Lobbying into Your Federal Sales Strategy

Gene Moran, PhD

Routledge
Taylor & Francis Group

A PRODUCTIVITY PRESS BOOK

Designed cover image: Shutterstock

First published 2024
by Routledge
605 Third Avenue, New York, NY 10158

and by Routledge
4 Park Square, Milton Park, Abingdon, Oxon, OX14 4RN

Routledge is an imprint of the Taylor & Francis Group, an informa business

ISBN: 9781032594828 (hbk)
ISBN: 9781032594811 (pbk)
ISBN: 9781003454885 (ebk)

DOI: 10.4324/9781003454885

Typeset in Minion Pro
by codeMantra

To Our Grandchildren; May They Embrace Lifelong Learning

Contents

Introduction

In their 1981 book, *The Iron Triangle: The Politics of Defense Contracting*, Gordon Adams et al. describe President Eisenhower's concern for the emergence of a "military-industrial complex." The term foreshadowed the associated "iron triangle," the evolving inter-relationships of industry interests, committees of Congress, and the executive branch's agencies. Eisenhower first used the term military-industrial complex in 1961— *50 years later, the term lingers!* However, the condition to which it refers, the tension of competing interests, is as much a product of the failure of companies to participate in an open process as it is of industry giants ruling the playing board of federal spending.

There are three categories of lobbying in the United States: those that lobby, those that lobby but don't think they lobby, and those that don't. Research confirms companies that lobby Congress perform better in terms of size and type of contract outcomes.[1] There are well over 1 million companies in the US industrial base, a tiny fraction of which use the representation of registered lobbyists who might help influence and shape more favorable outcomes.

Some of the top industries participate in lobbying, such as pharmaceuticals, oil & gas, and insurance, as measured by lobbying spending. Perhaps surprisingly to some, the defense industry does not rank[2] even among the top 20 industries by lobbying spending. When ranked as one of the 13 sectors of the economy, the defense sector ranks 10th by size. In 2022, just over 12,000 registered federal lobbyists represented interests across all sectors; fewer than 1,000 represented defense interests. It's a curious dynamic—an industry not ranked among the top concerning federal influence spending has fewer than 10% of the registered federal lobbyists representing their interests. Yet when examining defense lobbying spending more closely, relatively few companies make this investment. In 2022, Lockheed Martin Corporation accounted for over 10% of all defense lobbying spending, $10 million of the $91 million total. Lockheed Martin Corporation was all companies' 15th top lobbying spender in 2022.

Defense represents the most significant portion of the federal budget annually reviewed and approved by Congress, with nearly one trillion dollars in the fiscal year 2023. Hundreds of thousands of defense companies compete for those dollars, yet nearly half of the defense acquisition dollars go to only 50 companies and their subcontractors. Thirty percent of those dollars go to just ten companies and their subcontractors.[3] As such, defense is a valuable case study to understand what may contribute to a concentration of winners that garner federal contracts. What can we learn from the defense industry about lobbying and its role in federal sales?

> Get Funded—Any company can learn by understanding more about lobbying in the defense industry.

It would appear something needs to be corrected. Or is it right, and you just don't understand it? What's unique about those top 50 companies? Yes, they are bigger, but that's not all there is to it. *They all lobby Congress* with focus and specific intent.

> Get Funded—The top 200 federal contractors across all industries each lobby Congress, yet defense industry lobbying doesn't even rank among the top 20 industries that lobby Congress.[4]

The US federal government is the largest consumer in the world, spending billions of dollars annually. The Department of Defense (DoD) represents the most considerable portion of the discretionary federal budget—the part that buys goods and services and is reviewed and approved annually—by a factor of ten! The attraction of defense's nearly one trillion-dollar budget can be irresistible to companies of all sizes.

If the market is so attractive, and lobbying Congress helps achieve better sales outcomes, why do so few companies leverage the lobbying opportunity to gain a better advantage? Some do but don't publicly acknowledge their activities and may need to be correctly counted in the fractional percentage I describe.

A well-documented category of lobbying known as shadow lobbying is associated with the what's known as the revolving door. A shadow lobbyist gains expertise while working in government, and then leaves government (via the revolving door) to work for a company directly or as a consultant, using prior senior-level government contacts. It's not a crime to use those great contacts. However, failing to disclose the relationship representing a commercial interest to *certain* senior levels of the federal government is a crime when the shadow lobbyist represents in exchange for compensation. Not all former government employees participate in shadow lobbying from their new corporate roles, but enough maintain a high-level dialog with their former agencies that the terminology of shadow lobbying exists and is evident in academic research.

The "Revolving Door"

The endless flow of news coverage contributes to a negative perception of lobbying. There are plenty of high-profile examples of the misdeeds of the powerful few allowing their avarice to cloud their duty to their constituency or clients. They quickly become household names: Congressman Randy "Duke" Cunningham (bribery, tax evasion, conspiracy—partially pardoned by President Trump); Congressman Chris Collins (insider trading—pardoned by President Trump); Congressman Duncan Hunter, Jr. (campaign finance fraud—pardoned by President Trump); and lobbyist Jack Abramoff (fraud, conspiracy, tax evasion), to name a few from recent years. President George W. Bush denied Abramoff's request for a pardon.

Government Deals Are Funded, Not Sold focuses on the third category of lobbying mentioned at the outset, those who do not lobby. It's easy to conclude the system is unfair, unlikely to change, and populated by well-connected insiders who move through the revolving door. *I said almost too easy.* Digging a little deeper, *Government Deals Are Funded, Not Sold* will reveal that the real challenge to more democratized access to Congress for all companies is within our reach—*if we could all only see it!*

Defense executives' perspectives of lobbying by those who face the decision to lobby Congress can run the gamut. Some can only see what appears as an imbalance of subsequent contracting outcomes stemming from "dark money,"[5] "soft money,"[6] large companies with more resources, the need for a well-placed sugar daddy,[7] Congressman or Senator, or worst of all, plain ignorance of how lobbying works. Given how news of both scandalous and above-board political activities often intertwine, it might seem reasonable to make such assumptions that lobbying is complicated, unsavory, and best left to the big guns.

I'll identify how the inability or unwillingness to integrate lobbying into a sales strategy stems from hubris, ignorance, and lack of imagination. Thinking, "I've got this," and relying on their wits and narrow networks, too many defense executives struggle to gain real traction to consistently win large contracts. Companies shy away from a dynamic they need help understanding and taking the time to learn. The result? The biggest winners aggregate at the top of the defense industrial base pyramid, while the hundreds of thousands of "others" are left to wonder what just happened and why it's so hard.

I have directly observed the defense lobbying dynamic from multiple perspectives for over two decades. For nearly 10 years, I have been an independent defense lobbyist helping companies of all sizes navigate Washington, DC's complexities and mysterious ways. Before my current role, I was a corporate lobbyist as a Senior Vice President for a principal prime contractor overseeing dozens of programs on Capitol Hill; a liaison to Congress for the US Navy in multiple roles as a senior active-duty officer; and a congressional staffer while on loan from the Navy to the office of the late Senator Thad Cochran (R-MS), a senior member of the Senate Appropriations Defense Subcommittee.

In my present role, I routinely participate in the budget, funding, and policy process and guide others to shape better outcomes for DoD, my clients, and our warfighters. Bringing forward credible information,

I know how applying facts, leverage, influence, language, and reason helps influence outcomes during the critical legislative phase of funding decisions. My perspectives come from my front-row seat, observing how some companies use lobbying Congress to support better outcomes for their company and the warfighter. I want you to understand how you can better access this essential element of government, regardless of your industry or company size.

Get Funded—There is no smoke-filled back room. Your opportunity is hiding in plain sight if you could only see it!

Throughout *Government Deals Are Funded, Not Sold*, I'll explain why lobbying can be a good thing, not a cause for concern. Unfortunately for all of us, most companies do not lobby. As a result, they leave an essential part of the funding and contracting process out of their strategic plan. The implications are insidious because others have already half-set the acquisition table when they participate in the subsequent contracting phase, where funds exchange for contracted goods and services.

So interested was I in this dynamic I focused my Ph.D. dissertation research on defense executives' perspectives on barriers to or facilitators of congressional lobbying. My research is the first to identify themes that shed light on defense executives' perspectives on lobbying. I'll explain how perspectives can dampen our views on the performance of our democratic institutions and the performance of democracy. *Government Deals Are Funded, Not Sold* can better inform any executive of things they can change in their actions and professional development that will allow their companies to thrive by participating more fully, competing more fairly, and winning federal contracts more often!

This being a book written for business executives, I won't labor to repeat my dissertation in full. It may be found in the scholarly databases for further examination. *Government Deals Are Funded, Not Sold* de-mystifies process, goes beyond the inflammatory headlines, and exposes lobbying's realities and opportunities of which any company may take advantage.

Gene Moran, PhD
Bradenton, FL
September, 2023

Notes

1 Ridge, J. W., Ingram, A., & Hill, A. D. (2017). Beyond lobbying expenditures: How lobbying breadth and political connectedness affect firm outcomes. Academy of Management Journal, 60(3), 1138–1163.

2 See www.opensecrets.org for a searchable database of multiple variables of lobbying, such as spending, industry, sector, and company.

3 Cox, A. G., Moore, N. Y., & Grammcih, C. A. (2014). Identifying and eliminating barriers faced by nontraditional Department of Defense suppliers. RAND Corporation.

4 See ww.opensecrets.org

5 Political spending by non-profit organizations that are not required to reveal donor lists. Some industry trade organizations fit the non-profit criteria.

6 Political contributions beyond the limits on individual contributions. Corporations and unions are legally allowed to make such contributions. Once made, the receipts of the contributions may be further distributed to candidates.

7 A Senator or Congressman with demonstrated abilities and willingness to influence funding

About the Author

 **Gene Moran,** founder and President of Capitol Integration, is the foremost expert on federal defense and security lobbying. He guides and advises defense companies of all sizes to dramatically improve federal sales through funding and policy change in Washington, DC. Thanks to his strategic advisement and proven methodology for success, Gene's clients enjoy extraordinary returns on investment. With 10+ years operating as a highly successful independent consultant, lobbyist and advisor, Gene's results for his clients are measured in billions of dollars.

The extent of his impact has seen Gene's policy initiatives implemented by Congress (in law), the President (in Executive Order), and the Executive branch (in agency policy and contracts).

Gene's relentless pursuit of innovation in his field has garnered multiple accolades. Spearheaded by Gene's leadership, his firm, Capitol Integration, has been recognized multiple times by Bloomberg Government as a Top-Performing Lobbying Firm. Gene is an inductee in the Million Dollar Consulting Hall of Fame® and a personal recipient of the prestigious Corrie Shanahan Memorial Award for Advancing Consulting (Consultant of the Year). Florida State University has twice-heralded Capitol Integration as one of the 100 fastest growing alumni-led Florida companies. He is also twice-recognized as a "Top Lobbyist" by the National Institute for Lobbying & Ethics.

Gene's groundbreaking academic research earned him a Ph.D in Public Policy and Administration from Walden University. His dissertation explored the impact of congressional lobbying on contracting and the performance of democracy. He also holds a Master's in Financial Management from the US Naval Postgraduate School and a Bachelor's degree from Florida State University.

As a retired senior naval officer, Gene offers an incomparable breadth and depth of expertise. He served his country for 24 years in the Navy, operationally commanding ships at sea, and working in Washington, DC. Gene's exceptional insights and vision were sought out by the senior most influential decision makers of the Department of Defense and Congress. Gene was designated a Joint Specialty Officer and Proven Financial Manager before eventually transitioning from active duty as a Captain.

His extraordinary accomplishments include overseeing corporate PAC (Political Action Committee) strategy and implementation for one of the largest defense PACs, achieving over $700k per cycle. In addition, his vast experience encompasses 5 years overseeing legislative affairs for a Tier 2 prime and leading global congressional delegations in support of international ministerial activities and oversight.

He is the author of *Pitching the Big Top: How to Master the 3-Ring Circus of Federal Sales*, which explores the intricate processes involved in federal sales, and co-author of *Million Dollar Influence: How to Drive Powerful Decisions Through Language, Leverage, and Leadership* with Alan Weiss. This book identifies examples of how to correctly apply influence in business and government.

Drawing on his unique blend of military service and strategic advisement, Gene developed and launched Capitol Currency[SM], the only comprehensive multi-modal learning experience of its kind. Capitol Currency[SM] is specifically focused on helping executives navigate the complex federal sales landscape.

His experience during transition from active duty to corporate was the inspiration behind *Make Your Move*, a book and podcast dedicated to helping veterans self-assess and address the challenges they face when charting their post-military careers. The proceeds from *Make Your Move* continue to benefit Freedom Fighter Outdoors, an organization which seeks to support injured veterans.

Gene is married to Julie and lives in Florida where they are avid boaters. They are blessed with four adult daughters and a growing extended family.

Gene continues to hold active security clearance and remains SCI eligible.

1

Why the Federal Sale Is More about Funding than Selling

Government contracting, GOVCON in the acronym-rich vernacular of Washington, DC, is a blend of process and probabilities. Hundreds of thousands of companies position for government opportunities by filtering the public announcement of those opportunities using keywords in the announcement database, the System of Awards Management (SAM). This crudest form of artificial intelligence delivers notifications to companies and their business developers, signaling that the government is interested in something that may closely resemble that company's product or service.

The public notice is a familiar request for information (RFI) and a request for proposal (RFP). They are the morsel of food that triggers the near-Pavlovian response causing a company to react to the solicitation by cranking out a proposal. The capture teams, long on experience and often less on broad process expertise, follow the formal methods of analyzing, scoring, reviewing, approving, and submitting a proposal. This process repeats dozens, if not hundreds, of times yearly in many companies using time-tested and widely adopted capture methods.

> Get Funded—In Washington, DC, it's not real if it doesn't have funding.

Only some executives appreciate how the funding that will pay for the contract moves into position. This critical shortcoming in business intelligence directly contributes to the consolidation of winners. Why? Because the business development team, and too often the leadership

DOI: 10.4324/9781003454885-1

team, needed to understand the simple concept: *it's not about the contract as much as it is about the funding of the contract.*

THE ALLURE OF GOVCON

The contracting process is so appealing because it's so close and available. It's directly within reach and takes little imagination for executives of business development and sales teams to foresee the fullness of the opportunity. The government describes a need and offers enough specifics in the public solicitation to allow a company to reasonably discern its ability to fulfill the solicitation's stated need. It sounds so simple, even transactional. The call goes out, multiple responses come back, and the government selects the best fit.

What needs consideration in this process description is how the funds make their way to the government checkbook that allows competition to occur. "Why does this matter?" you might ask. Why would the government ask the industry if they didn't have the money in place?

In the right situations, some homebuilders might build a home "on spec," short for speculation. They deem the conditions of an economy, a development, a neighborhood, or the health of the demand for housing strong enough to believe that the house will sell on completion, if not before. They start building the house without a firm buyer being identified. Sometimes government requests for proposals are effectively issued "on spec," putting a signal in the air to the industry with the expectation that funding will arrive in time.

One can filter the SAM database from any location with a WiFi signal. It is effortless. Enter the keywords of interest, and sit back until the solicitations arrive in your inbox. Some do no more than this and can generate enough business to keep the lights on. Most are trying much harder. But let's not get ahead of ourselves.

The government must publicly disseminate its intention to purchase something, with the idea that it provides all eligible companies an equal opportunity to participate in the competition. Where possible, the government buyer likes to have more than one offeror for a solicitation. Multiple offerors suggest that there is competition, and the most qualified will win through a discriminating and fair analysis. There are numerous exceptions, but the government will attempt to identify two worthy competitors before an award.

It can't be this simple, though, can it? The process described above is the tail end of a much more robust process that repeats as a perpetual cycle. The contract from competition among proposals signals the end of a budget execution process. The same execution process is also the tail end of a four-phased process. You thought you were standing in boarding Group 1 to board the contracting ride; you're actually in Group 5 or the standby list, and you may not even have a seat (Figure 1.1).

The Line Forms Here

There are plenty of books and professional writings[1] describing the arcane nature of federal budgeting in terms beyond the scope of this book. However, the government's Planning, Programming, Budgeting, and Execution (PPBE) process is required reading for any executive selling to the federal government. PPBE is a dated and much-maligned process intended to protect the spending of substantial taxpayer money. The PPBE process of programmatic budgeting dates back to the 1960s and, as of this writing, is again under review by another perpetual creature of Washington, DC, *a special commission!* Anticipated forthcoming changes or adaptations of PPBE will not change the fundamental nature of the funding process. Instead, the changes will be marginal adjustments to some mechanical steps in a cumbersome process.

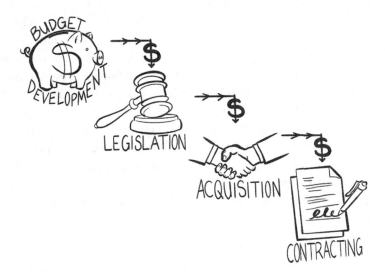

FIGURE 1.1
Four phases of the budgeting process.

Get Funded—The budget is more important than the elusive contract.

An understanding of at least the four primary phases of the budget process captured within PPBE is shown above and can point you toward where the line really begins. In simple terms, a need must be validated as a requirement. When a requirement is validated, it can then be positioned in relative priority for consideration in what will become a budget proposal. Each federal department creates a budget proposal that the President consolidates as a Presidential Budget request of Congress, referred to by insiders as PB. The budget proposal can take months to develop in some executive branch agencies; in defense, it takes two years.

Because a budget can take years to develop, there are multiple budgets in development or implementation at once. Developing, approving, and executing a fiscal year's budget is a cumbersome and lengthy process. Budgeting is in perpetual motion, with three years of budgets in some state of development, approval, or execution simultaneously. This lengthy process is good news for any business developer as the multiple budgets reflect near-, mid-, and long-term opportunities to influence the process *before a contract award.*

During the earliest phases of budget preparation, the budget process might seem opaque because it's not yet public. Public budget disclosure occurs when the budget goes to Congress. However, clues all around provide substantial indications of what the coming year's budget will include. For one thing, the budget that was approved and is being executed to contracts today offers at least a glimpse at future spending plans. Further, myriad associations hold conferences, ceremonies, and events where public officials can hint about their priorities and challenges in their public commentary. Congressional testimony is often filled with agency officials similarly commenting on plans, priorities, and concerns. A cottage industry of professional analysts, academics, and thought leaders monitor and comment on all such public commentary by sitting government officials. Subscription services[2] offer aggregated summaries and analysis of such public positions.

Get Funded—Official public comments reflect agencies' wants and needs, but Congress determines funding levels that fuel contracts.

Saturno[3] describes that the budget request, formulated by the executive (agencies and the President), is then evaluated, marked up, and approved as an authorization (policy) bill or appropriations (funding) bill that the executive branch will execute. The execution of the budget takes place through the acquisition and contracting phase of the budget cycle identified above. This budget development and congressional review process precedes the acquisition and contract phase by years, *in which any company could exert an influence on the process.*

FUNNELS, CAPTURE, AND COLORED HATS

A business opportunity funnel is a widely accepted visual that depicts the probability or readiness of an opportunity before it fully matures. A lead begins at the top of the funnel, and as conditions support, the lead is further confirmed and developed into a pursuit that may eventually become booked business. Cold leads are at the top of the funnel, and business ready to close is at the bottom. The government's ability to pay for the product or service bears on the movement through the funnel, but its significance is often underappreciated by those trying to close business. *Government Deals Are Funded Not Sold* will help any team understand how to dial up the influence of the necessary funding sooner than later.

Capture management in pursuit of federal opportunities has matured into a form of art. Yet another cottage industry exists to lend critical and specialized capture support to companies of any size. Experts can be hired as contractors or brought in-house as full-time employees in the most prominent companies. Integrated software helps manage the substantial amounts of information a capture team will sift through and exploit in designing its capture plan. Key points such as identification of decision-makers, technology maturity, the strength of field support, and competitor's offerings are analyzed, weighted, and scored.

As companies formulate plans, corporate capture teams subdivide into smaller teams known as red hats and black hats, for example.[4] Each team will either play the role of a competitor or specifically attempt to discredit the capture team's plan. Doing so subjects the proposal to stressors and challenges the capture team may need to pay more attention to.

An early question a capture team will ask is whether the potential government customer has the money to buy the company's product. The question is perfunctory, and the answer is best and most often confirmed by looking at the approved appropriations bill for the current fiscal year. Too many companies don't know how to find this publicly available information[5] on their own. They may incorrectly assume that since a proposal request is public, the funding must be in place. It's only sometimes the case.

FUNDING MAKES THE OPPORTUNITY REAL

NHL hockey all-star Wayne Gretzky famously stated that he "skated where the puck was going, not where it has been." It's a great line and perfectly captures his enduring capacity to pull off miraculous shots by outmaneuvering his opponents. But government contracting isn't hockey, and skating to where there is no funding makes no sense. To continue the metaphor, you want to work to get funding in place, and then carefully protect it by shaping requirements and specifications that will eventually yield a contract. Too many industry executives chase shiny objects with insufficient funding in place and, therefore, *effectively skate to an empty place on the hockey rink of federal sales.*

There are multiple ways to help the government customer position funding or adjust policy so funding will be otherwise made available. Some methods that I'll identify in more detail later in the book include the following:

- Helping the customer recognize the need is deserving of designation as a requirement. Knowing this need helps position you from the outset of the budget process—*but this is also the longest path to a contract.*
- Partner with an established prime partner with contract vehicles in place with your desired federal customer. The credibility of an established prime and ease of the contracting burden simplify things for the acquisition officials charged with contracting your capability. This relationship can move you along faster.

- You can educate and inform congressional decision-makers about why your capability should be funded by Congress even if the executive branch agency has yet to identify funding in their agency in the budget. This preparation in the legislative phase allows you to skip a year or more of bureaucratic evaluation by the agency.
- Requesting funds already approved for one purpose be reprogrammed to your capability during the year of budget execution. For many reasons, programs don't always perform to cost and schedule, and it can make sense for the government customer to move funds.[6] This funding option is the closest to you and can produce an up-side sale you have yet to forecast in the current year.
- Helping the government customer craft policy or Congress to craft legislation that subsequently informs policy.

Some extremely dynamic sales people are known for their interpersonal skills, professional contacts, and gifts of influence and persuasion. Charm and charisma help; however, funding is the essential ingredient. Even Wayne Gretzky, "the great one," couldn't make a puck materialize out of thin air.

SUMMARY

The version of GOVCON extant in the defense industry exists throughout the government and industry dynamic and can be found across all agencies of government. Throughout Chapter 1, I've hammered home that funding stems from a more complex budget process. You don't need to be an expert with green eye shades to appreciate the significant muscle movements of the budget process. But it would be best to become more expert at knowing the exact status of funding that affects your product or service. Knowing where funding decisions originate and how they rank can also present opportunities for you and your company to influence and shape outcomes. As identified in the introduction, the most successful federal contractors understand this dynamic and fully participate throughout the budget process, not just during the contract competition. In Chapter 2, I'll describe lobbying in specific detail and dispel myth and folklore surrounding the concept of smoke-filled, bourbon-fueled, back-room deals.

NOTES

1 Such as: Saturno, J. V. (2020). *Introduction to the Federal Budget Process*. www.crs.gov.
2 See Bloomberg Government, Inside Defense, McAleese & Associates, and Politico for example.
3 Saturno, J. V. (2020). *Introduction to the Federal Budget Process*. www.crs.gov.
4 The hat colors and associated roles of capture teams continue to evolve. These are just two examples.
5 See https://comptroller.defense.gov/Budget-Materials/, https://www.appropriations.senate.gov, or https://appropriations.house.gov/legislation, for example.
6 There are formal limits to the reprogramming of funds. In FY23, amounts above $10 million are considered "above threshold" and must be formally approved by the four congressional defense committees: SASC, HASC, SAC-D, and HAC-D.

2

Lobbying

The act of lobbying involves written or verbal communication with relevant congressional and executive branch decision-makers to influence outcomes. Protected in the Constitution's First Amendment "right of redress of grievances," lobbying is a right afforded to all citizens and dates back to the earliest days of our government. In its landmark Citizens United vs. Federal Election Commission, the Supreme Court effectively extends personhood to corporations while recognizing campaign contributions as a form of free speech—more on where contributions fit later in the book.

> Get Funded—Legend identifies the term lobbyist originating with then-President Grant becoming frustrated during his moments of respite with a cigar and brandy in the lobby of the Willard Hotel.[1] President Grant referred to the petitioners who interrupted him as "those damn lobbyists."

Economists refer to lobbying as a rent-seeking activity that seeks to improve outcomes such as funding or policy without making an additional contribution. In fact, "pay to play," making a specific contribution or payment in exchange for a political outcome, is against the law. However, variations of influence can shape both law and policy. Lobbying is a skill one must learn by doing; no lobbying school exists. Successful lobbying requires an executive to understand the rules and processes at play while communicating a compelling message in a well-orchestrated manner.

An overwhelming number of defense executives have a "School House Rock[2]" understanding of how Congress appropriates money. For example,

DOI: 10.4324/9781003454885-2

they generally understand that committees form laws through debate and consensus building. However, my research confirms the linkages of the influence of funding and policy decisions on the subsequent acquisition and contracting phase which need to be better understood. This critical lack of awareness reflects a learning point for any company selling to the US federal government.

In Chapter 7, I'll demonstrate more specific ways companies can lobby to achieve better outcomes with minimal effort. The lack of understanding prevents companies from participating in the process. By gaining an appreciation of where the lobbying opportunity fits into the budget and policy development process in the executive branch and Congress, one can make better sense of the lobbying decision.

Congress spends 9–12 months evaluating a budget that takes as much as 36 months to complete from start to finish. Plenty of budget and policy proposal changes occur during the legislative phase of Congress's review. Imagine where else you leave an aspect of your business unattended for one-third of the time in development. You wouldn't, but that's what over 99% of businesses selling to the federal government do.

Get Funded—Imagine if a football team were to attempt to play a game without using one-third of the field for the entire game. That would eliminate the option to run vice throw the ball. How many 33-yard plays do you see in a week of the football season?[3]

I'll describe some fundamental rules governing lobbying and how you might think about messaging and communications that could improve your outcomes. Making minor adjustments to message sequencing through a layered, persistent, and deliberate communication plan can change the game for any company.

HOW LOBBYING WORKS

Lobbying occurs through communicating an organized message from a specific perspective, told deliberately to the executive branch and congressional officials, intending to shape an outcome. The concept of lobbying dates back hundreds of years in England. Yet, the United States term associates with activities in Washington, DC, evolving since the post-World War II era. As government regulatory actions began to increase during the 1970s, such as oil and gas, airline travel, and automotive safety measures, corporations recognized the need to be present in the policy dialog.

Baumgartner et al.[4] well capture the tripling of the size of the Federal Register, where regulations would be available to the public in the 1970s, coincided with a more than doubling growth in federal agency budgets. A new era of government regulation that directly and negatively impacted business required more regular attention. Businesses began shifting focus to offensive and defensive policy positioning. Through the 1970s, corporate lobbyists grew over 10-fold from hundreds to thousands. The 1981 Economic Tax Recovery Act and 1986 Tax Reform Act proved watershed moments in corporate lobbying as corporate interests influenced the final legislation. Birnbaum and Murray (1988) tell the story colorfully in "Showdown at Gucci Gulch."

In 2022, there are now just over 12,000 federally registered lobbyists across all industries and sectors of the economy. Some examples of the multiple ways lobbying influences executive branch and congressional officials and decisions:

- By an individual. A company executive describes why a tax policy should prevail to incentivize a company's participation in an essential industry.
  - The individual may be an in-house employee, a contracted lobbyist/consultant, or a member of a lobbying firm.
- By a group. A union believes that a policy will negatively impact its members by raising health care insurance costs for the company and union members, potentially placing jobs at risk.
  - Many voices with a common message.
- By a broad coalition. The hundreds of companies comprising the Submarine Industrial Base Coalition (SIBC) support building more submarines annually for national security and efficiency for the industrial base.
  - Again, many voices with a common message.
- Third-party advocacy. Think tanks, thought leaders, and industry influencers speak, write, and publicly opine on various policy and funding options.

- Various points of view target decision-makers and decision enablers.

When a President's Budget (PB) request goes to Congress for approval, it reflects the administration's priorities. It is a political document drawing on ideology, assumptions, and subjective choices. The PB is the administration's effort to align needs and requirements with funding and policy outcomes. Given the extraordinary amount of time and energy in preparing the PB for submission to Congress, the executive branch agencies feel ownership and loyalty to the administration's message.

In today's Washington, DC, policy debates are perpetual and cover all aspects of life, our economy, and our global position, such as:

Defense	Insurance	Technology
Foreign Policy	Trade	Health Care
Business climate	Taxation	Housing
Environment	Energy	Finance

Many policies are subject to the annual review or on a cycle of every two to three years. The ongoing nature of policy dialog suggests that participating in the policy inputs is one way to ensure that positions get consideration in the outputs, the legislation that becomes law and guides agency policies.

Get Funded—Lobbying is how alternative options and perspectives come forward.

Thoughtful as it may be, the PB reflects the best effort at a consensus of perspective *within the administration*. It does not necessarily reflect the consensus of all perspectives. PB often represents some consideration of industry inputs, including product and service providers, technology developers, and manufacturers. The industry spends considerable energy engaging the executive branch directly and indirectly through trade association activities such as shows, seminars, and various think tank colloquia. Some activities constitute lobbying, others are mere influence, while others are more traditional and widely accepted business development and sales tactics.

When PB arrives in Congress, its reception can vary wildly depending on the party in power in the White House, Senate, and House. A divided government, where different parties control each branch of government or each chamber of Congress, often assures that the PB lands in Congress with a thud to the amusement of the opposition party. Two tensions suggested above, a potentially narrow view of an issue or need by the administration, and a failure to achieve true consensus in the executive branch, set the stage for Congress to put its stamp on budget and policy proposals. It is in the jockeying and maneuvering to be understood where business development and influence become lobbying. The law, described below, defines lobbying by the type of meaningful action as well as by the audience.

SO, WHEN IS IT LOBBYING?

Over time lobbying has been defined by law, as amended in The Lobbying Disclosure Act (LDA) of 1995[5] and requires specific disclosure of lobbying relationships.[6] Relevant definitions of the LDA warrant your working understanding. Certain communications with covered[7] officials in the executive branch and Congress are subject to a reporting regime allowing transparency of a relationship where an agent exercises influence for compensation. In the simplest terms, when industry communicates with agency officials of rank and title senior to the equivalent of O-7 (one-star general or admiral), any congressional staff, or the most senior of the federal executive service, with an intent to influence, a lobbying relationship may exist. Chapter 7 will go much deeper into relevant aspects of lobbying compliance.

Legal definitions further describe who a lobbyist (agent) may be, either an executive devoting more than 20% of time toward lobbying efforts or a compensated, contracted third party, for example. Critical features of lobbying include an intent to influence an outcome such as policy or funding, and a persistence of effort in doing so, typically two meetings or more. The LDA reporting regime allows the relationship between a lobbyist and an issue and the associated compensation from an entity (company, trade group, university) to be available in the public domain.

It is entirely within the law to communicate freely with government officials in hopes of influencing outcomes. However, doing so without adequately documenting such activity would mean that the public not only would not be aware, *they could not be aware* that a particular agent or industry entity was attempting to influence an outcome. It is an imperfect reporting system that relies on the lobbyist's self-reporting. Since its inception, the LDA has proven inadequate to curb corruption and mischief completely, and it has been modified every few years as issues or misconduct emerges.

Get Funded—Lobbying is a legal and regulated form of communication. Within prescribed guidelines lobbying communications and relationships are reportable and transparent. It's the failure to report where so many fall down.

TIMING, PERSISTENCE, AND VALUE

The budget process loosely described in Chapter 1 forces decisions by imposing various deadlines, wickets, and gates. Some dates that impinge upon decisions:

- The start of the fiscal year—1 October.
- The end of the fiscal year—30 September.
- Agency delivery of budgets to the Office of Management and Budget (OMB), usually before Christmas annually.
- Delivery of the President's Budget to Congress—first Monday in February.
- Beginning of a new Congress every two years.
- Biannual elections of every member of Congress.
- Election of one of three classes (roughly one-third) of the Senate every two years.
- The expiration of funding authorities; varies by the type of funding account within each agency.
- Committee hearings and markups are scheduled annually and updated weekly.

- Procedural votes and test votes in both the House and Senate whereby support is measured before a bill comes to the floor.
- "Recess" periods are more correctly defined as district work periods—long weekends or even the lengthier August break.
- Holiday breaks throughout the year.

None of the dates exist in stone. A few are written in the law (fiscal stop and start and budget delivery to Congress). However, the dates are more like collapsible barriers, adjustable with mutual agreement. Time is the essential management tool deployed in Washington, DC. I'll describe ways to use the clock to advantage later, but for now, recognize that the markers described above not only guide a process but also offer leverage points.

Because time seems always to be working against a budget and legislative process, the significance of the information exchanged during meetings holds value. It can be easy to rush to share an update, knowing that a processing clock is ticking somewhere—however, the cost of sharing poorly prepared or incomplete information increases with each process milestone.

Providing credible and material information at the right time and place carries the day. My 8-Minute Rule of Messaging^{SM} (Figure 2.1) is a surefire way to get your points in quickly, but more is needed to guarantee accuracy. Further, it enhances good credibility, but it won't create it. Accuracy and credibility are on you and the facts you bring to bear.

There are innumerable ways to bring value to a federal-level decision-maker. Do any of these fit into your current messages and communications:

- Alignment with a defined executive branch strategy
- Immutable evidence of a capability
- Demonstrable metrics proving the consistency of cost and performance
- Head-count data supporting the jobs impact associated with decisions
- A viable technology roadmap validated by a third party
- An actual product or proof of service, as opposed to "vaporware", conveyed *via* PowerPoint

FIGURE 2.1
The 8-Minute Rule of Messaging[SM].

Persistence implies consistency. As the budget moves through its various fits and starts, the message must convey to the new and most-relevant audiences reviewing a policy or funding proposal. Telling the story one way to an agency official and another to a committee staffer is a surefire way to derail your idea. Congressional committees use full-time professional staff who are professional staff members (PSMs)—experts in their areas. Further, they communicate regularly with executive branch officials over whom Congress exercises its oversight authorities. It may appear the right hand doesn't always talk to the left in Washington, DC, but don't be fooled.

YOUR INFLUENCE

Lobbying requires a degree of orchestration to realize influence. Above, I highlight timing and credibility as essential elements. Too many executives need to pay more attention to the foundational level of *process* knowledge required to take advantage of the underlying opportunity to shape outcomes. In our book, *Million Dollar Influence: How to Make Powerful*

Decisions through Language, Leverage, and Leadership, Alan Weiss and I describe myriad ways to prepare in advance to show up for an encounter with a decision-maker fully.

The key is understanding the organization, be it an agency, committee, commission, or office of a senior official. Everyone in government is accountable to a boss, a constituency, or the citizenry. Recognizing where those individuals fit into a larger organization will help determine how and where to exert your influence.

Recall from Chapter 1 that the critical federal processes that fit together include budgeting, legislation, acquisition, and contracting. Each relies on procedure. Budgeting, acquisition, and contracting are all executive branch functions. Legislation is a product of Congress, so I'll call it a congressional function. Regarding budget authorization and appropriation, budgeting is a shared responsibility between Congress and the executive branch. However, with Congressional approval, there is federal spending.

In some cases, legislation is specific to budget policy and funding, but numerous other pieces of legislation may also impact your business. Examples include policy bills such as tax, trade, transportation, and financial services. The appropriate point(s) of engagement are different for each and benefit differently whether the story is told by one or many. Your influence in lobbying falls into two categories: what you say and where you say it.

What You Say

My 8-Minute Rule of Messaging^{SM} is designed to tell any story in minutes, no matter how complex. It mirrors what Congress uses to convey information across offices and committees, the congressional white paper. A white paper is your story on a single sheet of paper and includes four essential parts that can be conveyed highly efficiently:

The issue—why what you are talking about matters. People have to care about an issue to gain traction and momentum. There must be a logical connection to a constituency, a requirement, or an identifiable need.

The background—how we got here. Why is this problem or condition persisting, what's been done up to now, and why must it be addressed?

The discussion—a review of the options that could be brought forward told in a way that positions you and your solution as the most logical choice.

The recommendation—what specifically needs to happen to implement your idea?

When you can tell even the most complex story in a matter of minutes, you demonstrate respect for your audience and keep them engaged the entire time. If your story starts to get wordy or complicated, you lose the audience and they mentally move on to the next event on their overloaded calendar. Using the 8-Minute Rule of Messaging^{SM} allows you to get your points across and give time back to your audience, the most valuable resource in their day.

Case Study Example: Where You Say It

As important as what you say is where you say it. Given the movement of a budget's policy and funding decisions, there are times and places when communicating with government officials makes complete sense or no sense! While the budget is being prepared in the executive branch, its details are not publicly available. Executive branch officials are prohibited from revealing specific details of a pending budget before it is officially released to Congress by the President.

That doesn't mean government officials won't engage with you to receive your inputs and suggestions, nor does it suggest officials won't publicly offer general commentary in public fora such as trade shows and panels. Your ability to influence executive branch decisions is governed by timing specific considerations such as budget delivery stages (in the budget phase) or the release of a request for proposal (in the acquisition and contracting phases). As the warning labels on sales promotions sometimes say, "certain restrictions apply." Timing a meeting to suit your travel schedule demonstrates your need for more understanding of your federal audience. They've categorized you before you walk into the room.

If you were to go to Congress with an idea on a subject about which the executive branch has not formulated a position, you're wasting your time and that of your congressional counterpart. It's common for small business owner to invite their local member of Congress to visit their facility. During a great tour and meet and greet with employees (also voters), a condition or shortcoming may be described for the Congressman. That engagement is very unlikely to move the needle on your issue. Why? Because it's shared in a setting where it will quickly be forgotten, when a staffer responsible for the portfolio of the issue may not be present, and the timing of the tour may be out of phase with the many processes described above.

SUMMARY

Lobbying is carefully orchestrated communications designed to influence a preferred outcome. Nowhere in Chapter 2 did I mention a back room, a smoke-filled room, gift-giving, or any form of transactional relationship. Those myths stem from a long-past era that does not exist within the current law. The Lobbying Disclosure Act (LDA) is imperfect yet continually subject to amendment. Someone crosses the well-defined lines every few years, and Congress amends the LDA every few years. In place for 30 years, the LDA has proven an effective tool in providing public reporting and definitions of specific relationships between companies, government agencies, and officials.

Lobbying influences the perpetual and inter-related processes of government and requires a well-conceived communications plan considering both timing and relevance. Taking place in plain view and equally available to everyone, lobbying can be an accelerant to more favorable outcomes. The myth and folklore of lobbying keep the majority of companies from looking beyond the salacious headlines and understanding opportunities within their reach. In Chapter 3, I'll explore how your lack of awareness may be suppressing your sales, while high awareness levels could fuel your sales.

NOTES

1 See: https://washington.intercontinental.com/history/. This legend has been debunked elsewhere; see: http://www.welovedc.com/2009/06/09/dc-mythbusting-lobbyist-coined-at-willard-hotel/.
2 For those under age 60, School House Rock was a collection of televised animated musical segments designed to help children learn how their world works.
3 In 2022, the average yards-per-play of the top three NFL teams was 6.4 yards!

4 Baumgartner, F. R., Berry, J. M., Honjacki, M., Kimball, D. C., & Leech, B. L. (2009). *Lobbying and policy change: Who wins, who loses, and why.* University of Chicago Press.

5 See: https://www.senate.gov/legislative/Lobbying/Lobby_Disclosure_Act/TOC.htm.

6 2 USC Ch 26, Disclosure of Lobbying Activities.

7 See: https://www.senate.gov/legislative/Lobbying/Lobby_Disclosure_Act/3_Definitions.htm.

3

You Don't Know What You Don't Know

The federal budget process is a daunting, multi-year journey that begins from the bottom of every agency (Army, Navy, Customs and Border Protection, *etc.*) with a crude forecast of conditions each agency will operate in three years. Think about that. The federal funds obligated today conform to some degree with a plan someone (or some series of committees) began tooling three years ago! It is insanity, and this process contributes to poor decisions that comptrollers and program managers must make as conditions unfold in ways that were not accurately forecasted.[1]

Recall from Chapter 1 that budgeting is one of the four processes that fit together, and the other three being the legislative, acquisition, and contracting processes. They all require substantial working knowledge for companies to participate fully. Communicating with Congress during the legislative phase is also a process. As described in Chapter 2, congressional communication is, by law, lobbying. Acquisition and contracting are best known to the industry, and executives' awareness levels are higher in these two phases and associated processes.

Get Funded—The masters of the four processes run the tables in federal sales.

Two-thirds of the budget's development time is in the executive branch, and one-third in the legislative branch (Congress). Several factors contribute to executives' limited understanding of Congress's role in funding and policy and hamper what could and should be better outcomes for all companies. This chapter begins to expose perceptions of facilitators and barriers to lobbying Congress.

DOI: 10.4324/9781003454885-3

Throughout this chapter, and onward through Chapter 9, I will include elements of my research of defense executives' perspectives on lobbying Congress. My research focuses explicitly on *perceived* facilitators of and barriers to lobbying Congress. Using widely accepted qualitative research techniques, I conducted semi-structured interviews with defense executives who were in a position to oversee their company's decision to lobby Congress. Coding software allowed me to dissect the interviews and subsequently identify themes present in the subjects' responses that give broader meaning to the responses when viewed collectively.

I won't drag you into the weeds of research methods. This book is a business book, not an academic report, so I'll present only the research highlights to offer sufficient texture. However, all industries can learn from the defense industry examples of how they work on the processes or don't. I'll supplement academic research findings with my observations and lessons learned in the defense and lobbying industry for 20 years. You'll see parallels from the defense industry that are likely present in your industry; a focus on the tail end of the contracting phase or a rush to respond to a Congressional proposal well after it has gained momentum (and press coverage!).

Get Funded—At the top of the list of coded themes to emerge in the research is the presence, or lack, of awareness.

The awareness theme dominates my research, appearing ten times more often than any other theme. Interview responses generated words and phrases that overwhelmingly suggest that the presence of awareness and lack of awareness directly affect an executive's perspective on lobbying and, to a lesser extent, on the broader aspects of budgeting (programming and execution). Awareness includes an executive's ability to synthesize complex, but hardly complicated, conditions affecting federal engagement.

Examples of the complexities executives face include elements of the budget cycle, lobbying knowledge, experience, connections, appropriations, authorizations, networks, working with Congress, and colors of money. High executive awareness of these concepts suggests that awareness facilitates the decision to lobby Congress.

Two sub-themes are part of the awareness theme: process and communications and connections. Process refers to both the process of funding through legislation (authorizations and appropriations), and the process of lobbying. Each requires an executive's working knowledge of these two processes to synthesize a vast array of environmental factors that all impinge on federal sales and policies that affect federal sales. Conversely, low levels of executive awareness present a barrier to lobbying Congress.

> Get Funded—Too many executives who rely on the federal government for either their sales funding or favorable policies that allow for sales don't know what they don't know. Lack of awareness is far more common than having awareness.

THE BUILDING OF A BETTER BUDGET

So complex and cumbersome is the Planning, Programming, Budgeting, and Execution (PPBE) process, the formal name of the defense budget process, that it can no longer keep up with the pace of technological change or the speed at which decisions unfold in today's world. PPBE dates to the 1960s when the hierarchical organizational structure was popular, and concerns over control of spending large sums of taxpayer dollars required a series of programmatic controls. It is truly a relic of the past.

In 2022, Congress directed that a commission looks at ways to improve the PPBE process. The commission's suggestions and improvements will take years, if not a decade or more, to implement. In the interim, the government's flawed PPBE process creates room for those who take the time to understand the peculiarities of the budget process and participate in it, knowing that the flaws create opportunities. It's not just that the mechanics of the process are flawed; executive understanding of the process needs to be improved.

UNDERSTANDING THE BUDGET PROCESS

While interviewing prospects when they first come to work with me, I ask company leaders to tell me what funds their contract(s) or program(s)—the majority struggle with this straightforward question. The question is somewhat open-ended and is answerable in multiple ways. In the case of a company that provides the content to US Navy aircraft carriers, some correct answers might include the following:

- "The US Navy aircraft carrier program office"
- "NAVAIR [the systems command that overseas aviation-related acquisitions]"
- "The Shipbuilding Conversion, Navy (SCN) CVN-80/81 budget line"
- "A program element number specific to an RDTE, N[Research and Development, Navy] budget line"
- "The defense appropriations bill"
- "The prime contractor, Newport News Shipbuilding"

Each response might be technically correct and suggests some connection to a specific place in a budget document, a finalized legislation approving a budget request, or a company or place that pays their invoice. But the responses must reveal understanding rather than confirm a need for more awareness. Most prospective clients need help to correctly answer this question in our earliest communications as I determine their state of alignment with the budget process.

Responses in my research of defense executives confirm the same anecdotal observations in that over half of the respondents could not specifically and correctly name where in the budget their funding comes from. Replies from my research run the gamut. Some were close to correct with responses like these:

- It's almost all RDT&E [Research, Development, Test & Evaluation] and O&M [Operations & Maintenance], probably, and some procurement funding. Yeah, I guess we get all three."
- Appropriated dollars, RDT&E [Research, Development, Test & Evaluation]."

The majority could/did not respond correctly, or sheepishly acknowledged they didn't know for sure where their funding comes from, replying, "not with a lot of certainty," for example.

Do you know where your funding for your programs fits in the budget? Are you in the majority? The odds suggest that both you and your competitors don't know enough about the budget process. It's not your fault, but what you do about it is within your control.

> Get Funded—It ain't what you know that gets you in trouble. It's what you know for sure that just ain't so.
> ~*Mark Twain*

Suppose you don't know where your program's funding resides in the budget. In that case, there is no way to track its durability over the years as the request for funds moves through the agency customer, to OMB, then over to Congress, and then back to the agency customer. Cuts, adds, adjustments, changes in priority, congressional marks, and reallocations can all apply to your funding lines.

The ramifications translate to an unmet expectation—you could wait a year or more thinking your opportunity is coming, only to learn too late that the funds were cut or moved much earlier in the process. If you don't know what you're looking for in terms of early indications and warnings, as well as when and where to look, you are reacting to the monolithic budget process instead of driving outcomes.

> Get Funded—"There are known knowns—there are things we know we know...We also know there are known unknowns—that is to say, we know there are some things we do not know...But there are also unknown unknowns, the ones we don't know we don't know."
> ~*Donald Rumsfeld*

The budget process does not contain unknown unknowns. It is true that the precise details of the budget process are sequestered during its early development and are only public once the President sends it to Congress. Those would be known unknowns in that we know the budget is being developed within the executive branch agency; we just don't know what's in it.

However, many of the budget's details are known unknowns. They are understandable through careful analysis of executive branch officials' orchestrated public comments, including strategic documents, keynote speeches, and participation in industry-led seminars and colloquia. Further, close relationships with resource sponsors and program managers, including their staff, are constructive. In the defense community, this knowledge comes from "customer intimacy," the close relationship and understanding of the customer's needs, situation, *and ability to pay you.*

While the budget moves through Congress, committees reveal marks to the President's budget request. After the completion of hearings leading up to a committee markup, committees will publicly reveal their mark on the proposed budget request. The respective House and Senate committees will go through similar processes while getting to their bill versions. In defense, those four key committees are House and Senate Armed Services Committees (HASC and SASC), and House and Senate Appropriations Defense Subcommittees (HAC-D and SAC-D). At this point, the budget contains known knowns. We know what the President requested and what the committees think of the request in precise detail. The legislative marks are released to the public as the process unfolds and the legislation moves through floor votes and conferencing between the House and Senate.

Their marks become public by the respective subcommittees, their full committees, and again as the bill moves to the floor of each chamber. Known knowns are evident at multiple points in the legislative process. Failure to appreciate how to track this process can significantly hamper an executive's *awareness* of how the future sale is unfolding during these budget development and review activities. Next, I'll identify how the misdeeds of the few may skew your understanding of lobbying before describing how the lobbying process can influence the budget and legislative process.

LOBBYING AS A PROCESS

In Chapter 2, I began to describe what lobbying is, how it's defined, and the various approach channels such as an individual in-house corporate lobbyist; contracted support hired to help a company; a coalition aligned to a common issue; or third-party advocacy communicating a position from an arms-length such as Op-Ed pieces, articles, or social media campaigns. The relevant audience of lobbying activities through any of these channels is those government officials with authority to make decisions or the enablers and influencers who surround those same decision-makers. Lobbying is about presenting relevant and timely information necessary to form decisions.

In 2016 Conor McGrath wrote of Lester Milbrath's 1963 seminal work on lobbying, *The Washington Lobbyists*, that Milbrath had correctly identified enduring characteristics of lobbying as a necessary form of communication. Milbrath studied the mechanics and practical aspects of lobbying, and his findings endure nearly 60 years later, having withstood the tests of scholarly research as well as the tests of life. However, today's executives tend not to see lobbying through as clear as a lens. It's no wonder why. Let's review.

The Misdeeds of the Few

High-profile personal failures make for great press headlines, internet clickbait, and breaking news, generating the impressions so critical to the revenue model of today's news flow. Unfortunately, the cruel headlines lead too many to believe that the misdeeds of the few represent business as usual. The Lobbying Disclosure Act (LDA) proved ineffective in thwarting lobbyist Jack Abramoff from charging exorbitant fees to his clients unfamiliar with lobbying norms and linking policy and funding outcomes to campaign contributions. Further, several members of Congress allowed their avarice to cloud their responsibility to their office and constituents. In each case, crimes were committed and charged, and the offenders went to prison. But the aftermath of the scandals paints lobbying with a broad brush.

The Honest Leadership and Open Government Act (HLOGA) was passed in 2007 to close several loopholes associated with the revolving door of Senators and Representatives leaving office and becoming lobbyists. Cooling-off periods for members of Congress and the senior-most executive branch officials require those officials to wait one or two years before using their government connections to wield influence in a new corporate role. Rules would restrict gift-giving, meals, and other professional courtesies in congressional settings. The "toothpick test" would represent the hand-passed snack now "allowable" at a reception instead of a dinner at The Capital Grille.

An earmark moratorium established by Congress in 2008, preventing members of Congress from directing specific funding to their districts, stemmed from President Obama's campaign for high office. Further, the Justice Against Corruption on K Street, known as the JACK Act, would pass in 2018. It was a high-profile two-page piece of legislation aimed directly at Jack Abramoff, who had failed to learn his lesson in jail the first time and was convicted a second time for lobbying violations.

The periodic uproar associating lobbying with corruption and bad actors, occurring every two to four years since 2006, leaves those unfamiliar with

Washington, DC, with the impression that everything is corrupt. Money must be filling every pocket in Washington, DC, right? That's hardly the case. Criminal cases are sporadic and certainly not more common than those found in other industries. That doesn't make the unethical activities right, but the negative perception has been seriously over-hyped. The Government Accountability Office (GAO) conducts an annual review of lobbying disclosure reporting, using randomly selected required filings of lobbying relationships and consistently finds lobbying reporting compliance above 90%.[2]

The Effect

Knowing little of the details of lobbying, executives tend to shy away from it. One research participant, a small company CEO, responded to a question about how one might lobby with, "No. I don't even know how to do that. I mean, we are a technology people at heart, so we don't really know how to play that game." The dismissive use of the word 'game' matched the body language of "I wouldn't touch that with a ten-foot pole." Executives unfamiliar with lobbying process details tend to demonstrate a similar reluctance to engage. They don't know how lobbying works, but what they hear is not good, so they say, "no thanks." In this scenario, executives choose to be unaware based on incomplete understanding.

I regularly speak at The Defense Leadership Forum, which connects industry with the federal contracting process and contracting officials. Most of their events occur well outside the beltway of Washington, DC, and serve to bring resources to company leaders who want to break into federal contracting but have yet to figure it out entirely. I ask audience members a fundamental question about lobbying, "How many federal lobbyists do you think there are?" The answers range from 70 to 75,000! *As mentioned, there are roughly 12,000, fewer than 1,000 for defense issues.*

Those company executives are not alone in their ignorance. When I ask the same question of lobbyists, even in private conversation, most of them are off in their guess at an answer by a factor of ten. We would believe that lobbying is both harmful and rampant. It is neither. While the number of federal lobbyists isn't specifically relevant to an individual company, the range of responses confirms a lack of awareness of the industry reinforced by public perceptions.

Some Understand the Opportunity

Despite some negative perceptions of lobbying, plenty of companies have learned about the lobbying process or have determined that it is a skill-set they can hire. Another small company president participating in the research stated, "I don't think lobbying is one of those skill sets you learn from watching YouTube videos and go to courses. It is so personal and it is so opaque that it's one of the things you kind of have to get on the inside and start doing it to understand how it really works."

Yet another research participant identified the value of a lobbying strategy first, "You really do have to lobby to get the condition set to even be able to sell in [federal]." Continuing, "and obviously the lobbying for appropriated dollars, it's kind of another different business there, but I think it ends up, for a lot of companies I think they find that beneficial."

Case Study

One research participant, a President of a cybersecurity company who came from the government before forming his business, recognized that the slow-moving government processes make the introduction of innovative capabilities challenging. He understood that getting the policy right matters a lot in setting sales conditions.

"It's actually for us in our business, is working with Congress for changes in policy around cybersecurity. Because what happens is as a company like ours tries to bring an innovative new capability to the market, we're often limited by poorly written policies that are usually based off of poorly written laws, which are snapshots in time of capability. So, you kind of write a law saying here's how you do cybersecurity, but then the cybersecurity ecosystem changes, but the law is still in place. So, government organizations are forced to buy out of date products. And so, changing the laws and the policies to enable more creative solutions rather than a compliance driven solution, I think is the right way to go."

The number of smaller companies participating in lobbying is challenging to determine. Although the LDA requires reporting lobbying relationships, identifying the details of the thousands of companies registered requires a multi-step process. Further, there is no way to capture the numerous companies that lobby but fail to register per the LDA. It would be an interesting avenue of research. We can glean from the hundreds of marks Congress makes to most legislation that they don't all stem from lobbying initiatives of large companies. Many are for amounts or in support of programs too small to matter to the large primes.

My business supporting companies of all sizes confirm that many small- and medium-sized companies also see the opportunity for congressional engagement. Clients come to me through referral by someone they know, trust, and like. They see others doing well by working with Congress and understand that engaging Congress can help. Still, they often need to appreciate the details of how to participate. They see competitors position themselves by securing supportive legislative language, a legislative funding increase, or a reference to their key differentiating element of a specification.

Following the Budget as It Becomes Legislation

As discussed in Chapter 2, lobbying is about exercising channels of influence with specific intent. Most lobbying intends to influence a more favorable outcome, whether pursuing policy or funding. Some examples might include the following:

- Shift the buying strategy of submarines from building one per year to building two per year. Doing so reduces the unit cost per submarine.
- Allow a tax benefit for companies that recruit and hire veterans. Doing so incentivizes companies to help veterans transition to meaningful civilian work.
- The Department of Defense must use modern digital tools to manage large programs. Doing so allows innovative commercial companies to bring the best technology into government.

These purposely straightforward examples allow the reader to appreciate that each issue has an executive branch and congressional component. A legislative proposal such as the three above can originate from an executive branch agency or industry with the agency's awareness if not concurrence. Industry can go straight to Congress with a proposal, but understanding the executive branch's position on the matter will be required. After all, these are co-equal branches of government.

Communicating with both branches is lobbying when communicating with Congress and may or may not be lobbying with the executive branch. How, when, and where a story is told with an intent to influence makes all the difference. What might seem normal business development and sales discussions are sometimes considered lobbying. Within the executive branch, executives often need to understand how this line is drawn. The definitions described in Chapter 2 matter. For example, communicating with a program manager (Colonel equivalent) is business development, while repeatedly communicating with a program executive officer (0–7 level general equivalent) is lobbying.[3] Some knowingly skirt the lobbying reporting and registration requirement (shadow lobbying); others fail to report due to simple ignorance of the law.

An entry point for communicating in Congress is a member's[4] personal office. It could be a member whose district the company operates in, a member of a relevant oversight committee or subcommittee, or one of more than 100 caucuses in Congress comprised of members interested in a particular issue, such as space flight or the National Guard, for example.

Some more essential forms of congressional communication include something other than back-and-forth dialog. Instead, positions in Congress reveal during events like hearings, member participation in industry panels, member floor statements, press releases, public markups of legislation, and commentary offered at fundraising events to a (trusted) audience of supporters.

Another small tech company president participating in my research recognized, "We were probably more inclined to be involved on the authorization act side because that's where the market space and the business conditions get tweaked. That's where they get adjusted." He continues, "There have been times we've been able to get the Congress to write some language, or request some GAO studies that have caused [change]…Now they haven't always corrected the problem, but we've at least been able to stem some of the bleeding."

COMMUNICATIONS—HOW YOU (AND OTHERS) TELL YOUR STORY

Emphasizing the quality of the message, the tech company research participant above continued, "Shaping a message that's going to resonate with the representatives you want to talk to certainly. Working with the lobbyist to craft that strategy, such that it's going to resonate…Developing that resonance, I think is really important." While this participant is clear on the opportunity, the specifics of how they'll engage with Congress and then follow the hearings and discussions are less clear. In this case, the research participant could articulate the need for help.

Salespeople often need to appreciate how poorly they tell their company's story. It can be particularly acute in federal sales, where process, timing, and flow matter so much. Salespeople often overcommunicate at the wrong place and time, with a poorly well-focused or well-delivered message. Using every minute of a scheduled 20- or 30-minute meeting with an agency or congressional official without leaving room for questions is the kiss of death. Further, "grabbing a few minutes to bend your ear" with a government decision-maker may merely add to the white noise they live with daily.

My 8-Minute Rule of Messaging℠ assures that the essential elements of your brief convey quickly and succinctly while allowing time for questions, or better yet, to give time back to the audience.

How the 8-Minute Rule of Messaging™ Works

It's essential to keep your message simple. It's ok if you have a complex issue, but complex does not mean complicated. Whether you are selling rocket parts or software, keeping your message from becoming long and complicated requires practice and forethought. Layering complexity as you go will keep your audience interested and engaged. But you must move along quickly.

Four essential elements of your story:

- The issue—Why are we here? Something is failing, lacking, under-performing, or costing time and money (1–2 minutes).
- The background—How did we get here? Briefly describe the flawed decisions, technologies, or unmet promises of prior choices (1 minute).
- The discussion—A brief review of what solutions exist and why yours is the best (2–3 minutes).
- The recommendation—Apply a specific amount of funding to a specific budget line, or change a policy to allow your solution to prevail (2 minutes).

When you follow this proven prescription, you assure your main points are delivered promptly and logically. You allow time in your meeting for some back-and-forth discussion. If you've hit your points well, you are likely in a position to give your audience time back in the calendar. Doing so assures you will get the next meeting if and when it's needed.

> Get Funded—You control the meetings you request. Come in with a plan; that alone will differentiate you from the competition.

Time is the overarching feature of decision-making in Washington, DC. Within agencies, rhythms of quarterly, monthly, and weekly meetings for internal needs leave little time to hear from outside companies. In Congress, the schedule of hearings, input deadlines, time for questions, floor time for debate and colloquia, and meetings have timing constraints. The clock forces a limit on the debate of issues. Understanding this underlying phenomenon is pivotal to the success of your communications.

Case Study

As a corporate lobbyist, part of my job was to bring General Managers of facilities around the country to meet their Senators and Congressmen in Washington, DC. As I sat with one GM over lunch before we began our series of congressional meetings.

Me: "Bob, how long do you think you need for your facility brief?"
Bob: "How much time do we have?"
Me: "The meetings are scheduled for 30 minutes."
Bob: "Then I need 30 minutes."
Me: "Wrong answer, Bob. We'll use eight."

Bob was hot that a DC guy was handling him. After all, he's the GM; he should be able to tell his story his way. Wrong. Bob was out of his element and needed to gain familiarity with his congressional environment. Bob failed in his GM role partly because he lacked awareness.

FIGURE 3.1
Align awareness of your capability across the 3-Ring Circus of Federal Sales^{SM}.

How Many Others Are Telling Your Story?

As described in Chapters 1 and 2, third-party advocacy, where others tell your story, can be helpful. Champions, who might influence or enable your proposed solution or offer throughout the decision process, can help amplify your message. Additionally, articles in relevant industry journals, newsletters, and newspapers can further shape your proposed story. It's the sequencing of the additional voices that can help tell your story through many voices (Figure 3.1).

Trade Press

In the defense industry, as with many industries, trade press report on more than news of contract announcements and government decisions on policy and spending. Traditional rules of journalism have morphed as information now moves faster and farther online than print media ever could. Multiple digital news outlets are driven by a revenue model that requires the generation of impressions—eyes on the content or clicks on relevant links. Impressions drive revenue for trade press just as they do for mainstream media.

Content placement has evolved into an art form synthesizing digital marketing, public relations, and sales. Paid placement of material in commentary, opinion, and multi-page stories and articles takes place throughout the defense industry trade press. For outlets that don't allow direct paid placement, nearly all allow for advertisement *via* digital tools such as crawlers, widgets, pop-ups, hotlinks, and banners. Any of these means can amplify the value message of a product or service, such as aircraft carriers, tanks, office supplies, and wearable technologies. With a relatively small budget, messages can reach hundreds of thousands of potential buyers *and decision-makers*. The reach can extend exponentially when the same content is reshared *via* social media.

Association Grassroots

Organizing multiple voices to convey a message calling for legislative action is a time-tested method to engage Congress. Multiple groups like chambers of commerce, the American Association of Retired Persons (AARP), and the Airline Pilots Association (APA) deploy grassroots communications nationwide yet focus on Washington, DC decision-makers. Annual "fly-ins" of doctors in white coats, autism advocates in purple shirts, pilots in uniform, or cancer survivors in pink demonstrate an unmistakable footprint when canvassing Capitol Hill in a single one-day messaging effort.

Segments of the defense industry are organized around platforms such as ships, tanks, and aircraft and use the same techniques but with much more focus. The Submarine Industrial Base Council (SIBC), around for over 25 years, routinely advocates for two submarines per year or funding support specific to the submarine supplier network. The Aircraft Carrier Industrial Base Coalition (ACIBC) advocates for funding for a minimum number of aircraft carriers to be maintained in active status in the interest of national security and the industrial base. Most large defense programs mirror this advocacy concept across their specific need and routinely suggest a specific number of platforms or a dollar amount be obligated.

Most aspects of our lives have some form of third-party grassroot advocacy representing us in Washington, DC—for example, insurance, pharmaceuticals, health care, privacy rights, and airline passenger rights. There are thousands of associations with a tuned message easily told by multiple voices. In my research, defense executives were aware that such forms of advocacy exist and even participate in them. However, none saw the potential of orchestrating such activity for the benefit of their own company. They could not see that an identical process is available, albeit at a smaller scale.

CONNECTIONS—YOUR NARROW NETWORK

It's more than just that your message needs more focus. Who do you need to speak with? Like most people, you'll ask a colleague in your network about how to connect or with whom to connect. That's likely the most accessible tool, but likely not the right one. In sorting through what connections and contacts might be needed, executives must synthesize environmental factors such as federal budget progress, legislative progress of relevant bills, economic and labor conditions, and supply chains.

Mentors

In my research, participants reference mentors and advisors as sources of knowledge to which an executive might turn for guidance. It's common sense that we'll turn to someone we know, like, and trust. In the defense industry, a mentor's guidance may be nearly exactly the proper support needed. That mentor may have faced a similar situation within or even the same agency program.

One research participant, a CEO of a services company, referred to "a long-term relationship [who] has helped me in the past." Another participant, a vice president of an industrial repair facility, identified, "so I had a mentor, a president of [a] company" to whom he turned for counsel. Yet another small company president providing electronics to the federal government cited "multiple mentors along the way" as resources he relied upon. Even in a homogenous segment of the defense industry like services, industrial repair, or electronics, the mentors sought had limitations in their levels of knowledge.

Consider the size of your current professional network. Does it measure in the hundreds, thousands, or even tens of thousands? LinkedIn caps the size of an individual's network. Let's face it, many of those people are not genuinely close enough to be mentors to whom you'd reach for confidential business counsel. Worse, the algorithms of social media networks and your own relatively limited diversity of background suggest that your network could be more diverse. There are over 300 million people in the United States and 8 billion people worldwide. Now, how narrow is your network?

Who to Talk to

Some executives in my research admitted that they did not know with whom they would communicate in agencies or Congress. In contrast, others knew they could turn to their network or an external contract lobbyist for help. Defense executives spend considerable time and energy determining with whom they must communicate amid a government audience that frequently changes positions and rarely publishes useful contact information directories.

Agency officials regularly participate in industry trade shows as speakers or panelists. However, some limit their exposure to the industry for fear of even the perception of sharing information they shouldn't or offering an unfair competitive advantage to a company. Mandatory ethics training intended to heighten officials' understanding of the rules and laws of industry engagement often scares mid-grade government officials into public silence.

Members of Congress and their staffs participate in public fora to a much lesser degree and generally prefer to talk business within the confines of their offices. Getting to know these members and staff takes both persistence and sophistication. In Chapter 5, I will describe how political giving can facilitate congressional discussion. Counter to popular belief, political giving is not required. What's required to facilitate good congressional engagement is recognition of why something matters or should matter to that member of Congress and their staff.

Get Funded—The most successful defense companies recognize that dividing responsibility for relationship management assures open channels for ongoing communications with decision-makers.

In the name of security since 9/11, public directories of email contacts for federal government officials remain mostly cloaked. At the same time, office phone numbers may have stayed the same in the preceding 20 years. Regular rotations of sub-cabinet-level officials from administration to administration present an ongoing challenge for executive engagement. Congressional directories with correct email addresses require a subscription to a service such as Bloomberg Government or KnowWho, and even those are incomplete. As with agencies, congressional phone directories of offices are generally available, although owners of specific issue portfolios require further investigation within an office or committee.

Rules and norms govern communications in the executive branch and Congress, each requiring varying degrees of sophistication that will reveal one's level of awareness. The government official on the receiving end can instantly identify an executive's credibility:

- Is the communication appropriate for the budget position or legislation in motion?
- Is the issue they present within the scope of the official's role and authority?
- Is the executive linking their discussion point to a government need or requirement?
- Is the message logically laid out per the 8-Minute Rule of Messaging[SM]?

Solving for the Narrow Network

Some executives in my research admit they needed to learn with whom they would or should communicate, whereas others knew they could turn to their network or external support for help. Though this perceived barrier was identifiable, nearly all research participants believed they could work through it. Company executives that come to me for support with their federal engagement openly acknowledge this gap in their federal communications plan. I help educate executives by identifying where, when, and how both process and message must align across the 3-Ring Circus of Federal Sales[SM] and the fiscal years of federal budgets. The alignment of the message requires awareness of the process and an understanding of how to best connect with the government audience.

CHAPTER 3 SUMMARY

Awareness captures an executive's abilities to synthesize a wide swath of high-level and environmental information, distinguish it from the ever-present white noise, and align with the complex federal sales landscape. It's complex but not complicated. Acknowledging the gaps in one's knowledge of the process, information flow, and relevant decision-making contacts is essential and requires honest self-assessment and reflection.

The most successful defense companies focus on resources and commit talent to coordinate the engagement of the federal process across the 3-Ring Circus of Federal Sales[SM] and the multiple federal budgets simultaneously under development. Companies whose executives have high levels of awareness of the processes and people associated with government decisions excel at higher rates than those with low levels of awareness. It may appear an obvious conclusion, yet, less than a fraction of 1% of defense companies participate in the formal lobbying required to succeed at this level.

In Chapter 4, I'll identify how investment is required and within reach to model the most successful defense companies.

NOTES

1 As of this writing, a Planning, Programming, Budgeting, and Execution (PPBE) commission is reviewing the budget process at the direction of Congress and proposing improvements to this arcane process.
2 See 2021 GAO highlights here: https://www.gao.gov/products/gao-22-105181.
3 Recall definitions of lobbying are clearly delineated and publicly available. See https://lobbyingdisclosure.house.gov/ldaguidance.pdf.
4 Unless specifically identified otherwise, I'll use the term member to mean Representative or Senator.

4

Outcomes

History credits Nobel laureate and economist Milton Friedman (from the 1960s!) that generating shareholder value is the primary reason for the existence of companies. In 2019, The Business Roundtable would suggest companies support stakeholder value, acknowledging how environmental, social, and governance considerations (ESG) have seeped into the boardroom. Let's agree that whether it's to support shareholders or stakeholders, the company must first stay in business. That means generating sales. Improved and profitable sales may be the outcome, but there are outcomes along the way that the most successful companies know how to monitor, shape, and influence in the executive branch and Congress.

Outcomes like confirming the need, shaping a requirement, and positioning in the budget must take place within the executive branch agency. Influencing those outcomes requires agency-level process awareness associated with budget development. Seeing those outcomes from a distance requires perspective.

Outcomes like authorization, appropriation, and favorable legislative policy occur in Congress, the legislative branch. While each is an outcome, the federal sale doesn't happen without each. Like with agency influence, participating in setting conditions for these specific congressional outcomes requires legislative process awareness (Figure 4.1).

WHAT OUTCOMES ARE YOU TRACKING TODAY?

There is a cottage industry of government contracting, affectionately known in DC parlance as GOVCON. (Only in Washington can meaningless

DOI: 10.4324/9781003454885-4

FIGURE 4.1
The multiple outcomes that mature in sequence.

acronyms be formed by simply merging letters.) GOVCON overweights the acquisition phase, where requests for information and proposals communicate sales opportunities through the System of Awards Management (SAM). GOVCON's focus on solicitation ignores the legislative phase and much of the budget preparation of the overall federal sales process.

Focusing on contract announcements and requests for proposals makes sense in the eyes of many, but often for the wrong reasons. Why? Because the conditions of funding, policy supportive of funding, and a position in the execution of the budget are not necessarily in place just because Uncle Sam issues an RFI or RFP. The government's public announcement process, where the government announces future opportunities, makes that part of the process look like the most likely entry point. After all, the next step after a contract is to receive a purchase order—that's as good as money in the bank, right? I said it could appear that way.

The ability of executives to link investment with outcomes is essential. As will be described in greater detail in Chapter 5, lobbying is an investment that supports desired outcomes, often with uncommonly high rates of return. Before exploring the necessary investments, agreement on the outcomes your business seeks must exist. Outcomes involve more than getting the purchase order.

Steven Covey once codified in his best-seller, "Seven Habits of Highly Effective People," that successful people begin with the end in mind. Prospective clients come to me, typically through a direct referral, searching for support with funding, policy, or advisement. When I meet with prospective clients, we gain absolute clarity on their objectives, effectively beginning with the end in mind.

Case Study

A typical exchange with a prospect might begin like this:

Me: Tell me what you'd like specific help with.

Prospect: Well, we've sold our night vision widget to the US Army for years, and we think the US Navy would also benefit from this product. Can you help us?

Me: Tell me more about why the US Navy should want your widget. Where would it be used? How does it improve their current solution?

Prospect: The US Army uses this capability as a soldier-mounted device, and it's also adapted to use on wheeled vehicles. The US Navy might benefit from using this in a base security application.

Me: Who have you spoken to within the US Navy?

Prospect: Nobody yet. That's something you can help with.

The prospect still needs clarity on their objective. They are applying sales intuition to a situation thinking that it should make logical sense—a new buyer (US Navy) should see the benefit of the capability and how limited the risk is since the product is already in use by the US Army. Sadly, many companies fumble around like this as they explore options to "grow the bottom line."

Many companies chase RFIs and RFPs, needing to consider their objectives. An all-too-common practice is for business development executives to set automated searches of the SAM database. As the government announces an opportunity, the executive receives an email alert to a possible match of a stated government need with a capability the company might provide. Again, users of this method must pay attention to the multiple years of coordination before the SAM announcement becomes public.

It can be satisfying to receive an alert of a potential match. Knowing the government wants something your company might provide can inject adrenaline into a capture team now able to focus on a specific demand signal from a government customer. Some questions you should have answers to by the time you think you have an opportunity in hand:

- Who is the real customer? Do we know them, and do they know us?
- Is the opportunity in support of a validated requirement?
- Do we have any relationship with the field users whose expressed need led to the requirement's validation?
- Is there funding behind this announcement?
- Which specific budget line, if applicable, by account and element number, funds this opportunity?
- Is this opportunity already identified for a competitor and being disclosed *via* SAM only to satisfy an acquisition policy associated with the competition?

The answers to these questions are entirely knowable long before the SAM announcement. However, because you may be focusing on the part of the process that's easiest to see, you'll miss early and essential information that should inform your approach to the opportunity. Let's step back from the contracting phase and examine some fundamentals.

Why Are You in Business?

The generation of sales stemming from contract awards leads to revenue. The revenue outcome sounds obvious. In federal sales, other outcomes contribute to the conditions allowing for sustained sales. Outcomes like contract awards, favorable legislative language, and favorable legislative or agency policy leading to improved sales are desirable. Sometimes we don't think about the conditions that fuel or inhibit sales, although we experience those conditions daily. "Buy America" is an example of a policy that might spur sales and inhibit sales depending on your supply chain. There isn't a perfect checklist for policies that help or hurt. *We know it when we see it*, to loosely paraphrase Supreme Court Justice Stewart Potter's attempts to codify a test for obscenity. But are you even looking?

Revenue with a sufficient profit to sustain is vital regardless of the company's construct or governance. Public, private, or employee-owned all rely on profitable sales. In my research, all participants indicate appreciation that outcomes like revenue are their company's raison d'être and essential to the business's success. It's the *linkages* of the precursors to a contract, such as legislation and policy, to the sales that produce revenue that confuse too many in federal sales. It would help if you improved how you link multiple process outcomes to your revenue and profitability conditions.

HIGH AWARENESS—SEEING POTENTIAL OUTCOMES

My research results reveal that executives with high awareness levels of the budget, legislative, and funding processes can foresee outcomes that contribute to a positive environment for their sales.

One participant, a president of a technology company, described how Congress could help new products or capabilities survive the critical transition from the development phase to regular funding through inclusion in a funding bill or subsequent budget. Support of such a transition represents an outcome that can last beyond the immediate fiscal year for a company.

In describing his understanding of the support that Congress might provide, this president said,

> As you're bringing a nascent program through the R&D [research and development] process, in my lingo there's what's referred to as the valley of death. It's the gap in between, let's call it a prototype and a fielded system, if you're trying to field a system...You're not going to get a whole lot of help getting through that transition from a prototype or a concept into full-on production...At times, without a little bit of congressional help, they wouldn't take the risk of seeing whether this program is truly going to work out or not. So that's a big one, is getting across that valley of death.

The same participant carried the research and development challenge further, demonstrating a high level of legislative process awareness, stating, "Those research and development dollars are very precious. If we've got something that we believe is for the good of the nation, raising some awareness and capturing funding for that is important."

Another participant, a Vice President of a manufacturing company, was cautious in describing what would encourage his company to participate more fully during the legislative phase of the funding process that precedes competition for a contract. He stated,

> "I mean, I suppose if there was something that we could tie direct revenue or direct sales to, if a program passed or got funded or continued funding, then I think there might be something there." His fourteen years in the defense industry had not convinced him of a repeatable linkage of outcomes to his sales.

Acknowledging the business discipline required to support the best business outcomes, a vice president in defense manufacturing described the companies that do best in federal sales, "...they're lean, they have low capitalization requirements. They [have] low infrastructure cost. They have pretty streamlined overheads. They have very low indirect cost structure, and they're able to win a lot of work." The inference is because those successful companies know where they are heading, they are able to put increased focus on business basics. They see the desired outcome(s) clearly.

LOW AWARENESS—CAN'T SEE THE FOREST THROUGH THE TREES

Another small business founder and president with relatively low process awareness described his approach, "I mean, it has to be something very large, very strategic for us to even pay attention at that phase." His words convey that the outcome must be so obvious that its potential is being openly described by media or the agency customer that there is no risk of a loss of required resources to his participation.

Another executive, a Vice President of a manufacturing company whose company employs outside lobbyists, recognized the value of engaging Congress in pursuit of desired outcomes. When asked for thoughts on how congressional engagement could hurt or help a company's competitive position, this executive replied, "The more I know about what's going on inside the halls of Congress, based on the intelligence I'm getting with my lobbying firm, then I can probably translate those into business strategies. And that's a competitive advantage." In this case, the executive recognizes his lack of visibility on parts of the process and uses external support to improve his awareness while moving toward preferred outcomes.

Executives with lower levels of awareness of the sales environment must track the essential phases of the multiple processes in motion to know whether they're tracking toward their outcome, profitable sales. When I ask prospects about the federal funds that will drive their annual financial plan, the responses can take several forms:

- "We've been growing 5% in the past two years and expect to meet the same growth at least this year."
- "Looking at the demand for our [widget], the [operators] love us and keep coming back. They tell us they hate [the competitor] product because of [a functional shortcoming]."
- "We've been the vendor of choice for [agency] for over ten years."
- "This technology is changing so fast, and we're [a number] years ahead of our closest competitor."

As I progressed in seniority in the Navy, I learned to "think outside the lifelines," applying ever-increasing technical knowledge of the ship's capabilities to the operating environment and the operational objectives. In my current role, I guide the most successful defense companies in helping their government customers and decision-makers flex their imaginations to see future outcomes outside their present field of view. In Chapter 3, I highlighted the process that yields intermediate outcomes. You'll need to improve your understanding of some budget and funding technicalities to recognize the outcomes along the way. To follow the money, first you have to know where to look.

Show Me the Money

"Show me the money, Jerry," was a classic line in the 1997 movie *Jerry McGuire* when Cuba Gooding, Jr. tells his agent, Jerry McGuire, played by Tom Cruise, the one thing his agent needed to do for him, "Show. Me. The Money," where the rubber meets the road. Tired of all the talk and red tape of agents and contracts, Cuba Gooding, Jr. delivered the clever tagline.

Cuba Gooding, Jr. won the academy award for best-supporting actor for his iconic portrayal of fictitious NFL player Rod Tidwell, in part due to this memorable scene. The player and agent distilled their relationship down to those four words representing how the service provider (Jerry McGuire) would demonstrate value to the client (Rod Tidwell). Rod Tidwell needed Jerry McGuire to do one thing, "show me the money, Jerry."

Looking for the money that may follow a contract and purchase order makes sense on the surface, and it's a trap many executives fall into. You'll have fewer surprise outcomes when you learn to follow the money and even help decision-makers position the money. It turns out that the movement of the money is hiding in plain sight in three particular places, each of which is publicly available:

- The budget request for the given fiscal year.
- The authorization bill for the respective agency for the coming fiscal year.
- The appropriations bill for the respective agency for the coming fiscal year.

Let's look at each to see where the clues and tells of future contract opportunities can be seen by anyone paying attention.

THE PRESIDENT'S REQUEST

Although the budget development for a future fiscal year takes as many as two years, churning through an internal agency review and prioritization process that takes place mostly out of view, eventually, the budget request becomes public as it moves to Congress. Just before that happens, government departments make an annual submission of their prioritized needs (as determined by a combination of internal agency officials and committees) to the Office of Management and Budget (OMB).

Before submission to the OMB, departments shape, consolidate, and prioritize the often-multiple agency inputs. The Department of Homeland Security, for example, is comprised of eighteen separate agencies ranging from the United States Coast Guard to the US Customs and Immigration Service. Each agency input also represents another intermediate outcome, yet your ability to influence this part of the process during this critical budget consolidation is virtually nil. You may have ongoing customer dialog leading up to this point. Still, during this period, roughly November through January, even the heads of agencies have only a limited view and are limited to responding to questions from the OMB.

The defense department budget, larger than the next closest department of homeland security by a factor of ten, is often subject to critical back-and-forth with the OMB on very large programs—the back-and-forth results in adjustments and trade-offs to individual service top lines. A US Navy destroyer costs $3 billion; adding one vs. two makes a difference, and sometimes those funds come from the US Army or US Air Force at this executive branch endgame. Other smaller departments like the Department of Education and the Department of Treasury come forward to the OMB with less fanfare and public speculation about what remains "in" or "out" of those budget inputs.

By law, the compiled budget inputs for the coming fiscal year move from the OMB to Congress as the President's Budget Request, known as PresBud, or PB, on the first Monday of February. In theory, this gives Congress eight-plus months before the start of the new fiscal year, October 1, to evaluate and finalize what will become "the budget." This February deadline often passes for various reasons that usually stem from election outcomes or political dynamics. Missing this deadline can immediately compress the remaining timeline to the new fiscal year. The fiscal year start of October 1 is a hard deadline that Congress regularly misses!

On whatever date the PB moves to Congress, it simultaneously becomes public. Press releases, summaries, briefings, and headlines capture high-level issues. Lists of "winners and losers" are quickly identified and circulated within the beltway. Websites for each department, and often individual agencies, publish downloadable and searchable budget documents that document the PB. The Department of Defense also submits extensive justification material to Congress in large green books, known as J-books. The justification materials spell out underlying decision elements for Congress to consider and are also public. Because these documents are public, they represent essential and valuable business intelligence for you and your team.

Federal sales business development experts devour and dissect the relevant sections of the President's Budget Request and accompanying J-books.

Ideally, the PB and accompanying justification can readily confirm what your business development team has already learned along the way from their ongoing government customer engagements. Too often, though, companies are surprised by what the documents reveal in this first public view. They might need to understand their customer's previously stated positions, feedback, or public posturing. Worse, your business developer completely misses this first public forecast of the future fiscal year's proposed spending because they rely on distillations from a subscription service or industry-focused media such as "Inside Defense," "Inside the Navy," or "Inside the Army," to name a few. To miss this fundamental public forecast is nothing short of federal sales malpractice. Yet, only some can point to the publicly available document that projects the intended funding of the budget line that funds their program, product, or service.

The PB evolves across the executive branch as a collection of agency and department outputs. In fact, PB in this compiled form now represents an input to the legislative phase of the overall process. PB is a political document because it's a reflection of the priorities of a political administration. For companies that missed their opportunity to influence the executive branch development of the PB, the only opportunity to make changes to the budget before the new fiscal year is through actions by Congress.

THE MARKUPS

Because PB comes forward from the executive branch, it's a reflection of the priorities of the administration, and it reflects the bias of the political priorities of that administration. Congress, being a co-equal branch of government, reviews the input of PB line-by-line and imprints on the priorities for each department and agency. Congress does this by transforming the input of PB into one of two types of legislation: authorization or appropriation.

Throughout the spring of each year, Congress conducts hundreds of hearings across all committees with oversight responsibility of the executive branch. Examples include Armed Services, Foreign Relations, State and Foreign Operations, Homeland Security, Appropriations, and dozens more. Some committees set policy *via* authorization bills, while others set funding levels *via* appropriations bills.

More prominent committees subdivide into subcommittees. The sub-committees sometimes oversee specific agencies of departments, but others often oversee various interrelated domains as diverse as trade, acquisition, or sea power. Chairmanship of a subcommittee overseeing SeaPower and Force Projection, or Tactical and Land Forces, for example, oversees substantial portions of defense spending policy totaling billions of dollars.

Committee hearings allow another public opportunity for executive branch agency officials and Congress to publicly state their funding and policy positions through questions, responses, or statements. Mostly, all hearings are open to the public[1] and offer essential business intelligence collection opportunities. Even if executives don't have the staffing or wherewithal to support attendance in person or by monitoring through C-SPAN coverage, transcripts are readily available online within 24 hours of a hearing. Searching for a hearing on US Army modernization plans might reveal any ongoing concerns about recruiting, use of technology, workforce development, or even your widget embedded in the new US Army wheeled vehicle.

That's right, your product or service may well come under review during a hearing where Congress reviews spending and priorities directly with your customer. Companies that are paying attention and participating may even have an opportunity to help members of Congress ask questions of agency officials that could influence the views of Congress on the value of their product or service to a particular program.

The hearings are both a forum for exchange but also provide an official record of the positions of executive branch officials (witnesses who testify) and the members of Congress who ask the questions. This record substantiates Congress' rationale for making changes to the PB. Following this part of the process, companies maintain a heightened understanding of how likely their agency is to receive support or a cut when the final spending bills are approved. This revelation is months or potentially more than a year before an RFI or RFP will appear from an agency.

CRAFTING LEGISLATION—MARKING THE AUTHORIZATION AND APPROPRIATION BILLS

During the hearing season, congressional committees also meet to review their relevant sections of the PB and consider where to apply changes in the form of increases or decreases to the president's request. The pluses and minuses are known as marks. Members of committees may raise issues for consideration on their behalf or behalf of constituents or fellow members.

Not every Senator or Representative can sit on committees relevant to their district, state, interest, or area of personal expertise. In these cases, members work together to look out for common interests. The interests are as varied as every aspect of our lives—insurance, health care, defense, or food supply.

Case Study—Non-Defense

The Red Snapper population has long been subject to management protocols intended to help sustain long-term fisheries. Fishing rights and commercial and recreational fishing restrictions in areas like the Gulf of Mexico impact fishing in all Gulf states—Texas, Louisiana, Mississippi, Alabama, and Florida. Similarly, in the panhandle of Florida, Apalachicola Bay, where a specific type of oyster can grow, is affected by water management decisions in Georgia and Alabama as water feeds into the Bay.

In these two cases, federal solutions supplement individual state efforts that only sometimes synchronize to the best outcomes. Support in the form of congressional legislative language and funding subsequently drives federal agency policies. Garnering committee support in situations like this requires members of Congress to work together to inform and demonstrate support to fellow members who sit on committees of relevance.

By combining awareness of an issue, understanding how the hearing process forces public positions, and use of effective communications with members of Congress who sit on committees or have access to committee members, more favorable legislation, policy, and funding decisions can be shaped. Shaped by you, that is. Companies participate during this legislative phase of influencing the markup process by telling their story consistently and thoughtfully by targeting committee members who care or should care about their issue.

Subcommittee markups precede full committee markups in both the House and Senate committees. The marks appear as legislation in the form of an authorization bill (policy) or an appropriations bill (funding). After passage by a full committee (authorization or appropriations), each bill moves to the floor of its respective chamber for a vote and then conferencing with the other chamber before final passage. Each step toward the final passage offers a more limited opportunity for final adjustments. Because these proceedings are public, each step reflects an intermediate and public outcome.

ONCE AGAIN, WHY LEGISLATIVE OUTCOMES MATTER

The final bills containing marks of increase or decrease to the president's requested budget (PB) are now stand-alone pieces of legislation. In defense, the specific program names, budget categories, and (if applicable) program element numbers describe specific funding levels or associated policies approved for the relevant executive branch agencies.

Eighty percent of success in life is showing up.

~Woody Allen

Companies participating in this critical legislative process have at least tried to influence outcomes to their favor (and presumably to the favor of good government). Keeping tabs on how legislation progresses and appreciating who is supportive or not supportive of an issue of concern guide their communications and engagement.

Low executive awareness of these budget and legislative interrelationships can prevent executives from gleaning the valuable intelligence that can guide their shaping of outcomes well before the acquisition phase begins. The most successful companies selling to the federal government are paying nearly as much attention to this part of the process as to the actions of their agency "customer." They do so because they recognize the value of the intermediate outcomes of markups. Participating in the process while authorization and appropriations bills are in progress will subsequently influence the coming acquisition phase.

> Get Funded—The top 1% of defense companies follow and participate in the hearing process because they recognize it's a second bite at the apple to influence a budget outcome.

SUMMARY

Maintaining perspective on the actual status of your future federal sales and your ability to imagine outcomes requires you to integrate your technical knowledge of government processes with your ultimate business outcome—profitable sales! This chapter describes intermediate process outcomes to which you've likely paid to little attention up to now.

I've specifically described the need to operationalize how you and your company follow the money in the earliest phases of developing the federal sale. By identifying waypoints in the integrated federal budget, funding, and policy processes, you can better tailor your company's tools and timing of communicating about your product or service. In Chapter 5, you'll learn how to appreciate the phenomenal returns on investment available in federal sales if you'd only start to see this expense as an investment rather than overhead.

NOTE

1 During COVID-19, in-person hearings opened the doors to virtual and hybrid hearings. However, during normal conditions, most hearings are open to the public albeit with limited seating options.

5

Investment

During my first sea tour, a Navy Chief told me, "There can only be one number one priority"—a sage observation from someone juggling multiple responsibilities. Corporate leadership demands such insight, but too often, defense executives prioritize investments haphazardly, succumbing to immediate pressures. There is only so much time, talent, and treasure to distribute among company objectives. Whether it's about hiring, research and development, control of overhead, marketing, travel, or participation in the outreach required of lobbying, investment decisions require prioritization. The internal competition for limited resources is ever-present. Lobbying requires a commitment to the investment over a lengthy and perpetual process.

My research results align with my observations of executives with respect to investment. Executives with higher levels of process awareness and understanding of the rules and policies of lobbying tend to have an easier time imagining the return on investment. Conversely, those with a less complete view of the overall process appear less willing to spend on what appears to be an uncertain outcome.

BUSINESS DEVELOPMENT

Most defense companies dedicate resources to business development (BD). While not precisely sales, BD is the process through which early communications with a federal customer typically occur, leading to an eventual sale. Executives with knowledge of their company's products and solutions look for clues across an agency or even across multiple agencies

 DOI: 10.4324/9781003454885-5

of government that indicate a potential fit. Executives in BD often receive compensation, in part, based on the outcomes of sales that eventually close because the executive found and "developed" the opportunity. Investment in BD, either with a full-time account executive, a team of business developers or through contracted third-party help, is required to generate perpetual federal sales.

Even small start-up companies need to figure out how to perform this required function and often go too long without committing to the investment BD requires. The most successful defense companies not only have teams of business developers but also invest in business developers with backgrounds or proven records succeeding with individual agencies and programs. Many defense business developers are former military service members with extensive relationships and operational and programmatic experience. For smaller companies, third-party support can be an effective way to establish federal connections and begin to connect the company to federal needs.

By definition, the business developers' focus on the federal customer tends to limit their view of the playing field to an agency or multiple agencies of interest. While this focus is essential, they often can't see for themselves or need access to reliable information about other critical phases mentioned throughout this book (budget, legislation, and contracting). A business developer focuses on the acquisition phase when funding for a requirement has long since been decided. Unfortunately, it often means that the business developers' understanding of industry and congressional relationships is less astute.

The most successful larger defense companies have other employees or teams of employees focused on budget development at the resource sponsor and program office levels of an agency. Further, those same successful companies recognize the value of having employees or third-party support helping to follow if not influence, the legislative process—lobbying Congress. Business development cannot succeed long-term without integrated information from these other phases.

Some typical shortcomings I see in business development:

- A Rolodex derived primarily from a prior position within an agency
  - *The narrow connections will plateau as government officials change position every two to three years*

- Lack of awareness about the capabilities of industry competitors
  - *Attendance at trade shows focuses on kindling of friendships as opposed to gleaning business intelligence*
- A poor ability to meaningfully differentiate an offering from the competition
  - *Lack of technical chops*
- Inadequate integration of publicly available business intelligence
  - *Lack of awareness of where to look and reliance on subscription services, headlines, and industry chatter*
- Inordinate pressure on generating a business win on a business timeline as opposed to the government timeline
  - *The compensation model encourages the wrong behavior*
- Inadequate understanding of business fundamentals required to support the delivery of a product or service on time and within budget
  - *Prior military experience does not equal business expertise*

When company presidents reach out to me for support, they fit into one of two camps concerning business development. One group believes they know the relevant government buyer well because they have prior sales with that customer, or they believe their relationship is unique (strong customer intimacy). However, despite their connection, they fail to sustain the perpetual business. In the other camp, a company president will know that their products' capabilities align perfectly with the customer's stated need, but they must align with the overall buying process. In this case, they know that their efforts are not working but must figure out why. In both cases, they have begun recognizing a need to invest, but I'll describe further that it's not just a required financial investment.

In defense, most business developers fail to recognize when business development in the executive branch is lobbying. As identified in Chapter 2 and will be addressed further in Chapter 7, there are specific definitions of lobbying and rules for compliance. Communicating repeatedly with senior government leaders in the executive branch, often PEOs and senior civilians, fits the definition of lobbying. Whether you call it BD or lobbying, both activities require investing time.

TIME IS MONEY

As the Chief told me in the introduction of this chapter, there can only be one number-one priority. Time is a non-renewable resource all executives must manage. When evaluating the performance of a public sector team selling to the federal customer, executives recognize that their time is as valuable as the resources they invest in people, capital expansion, and research and development. With limited time it can be easy to spend or invest it in areas where the executive sees the most significant return—the outcomes of Chapter 4. Therein lies a hidden problem.

The low level of process awareness (Chapter 3) inhibits the executives' ability to imagine preferred and better outcomes (Chapter 4), so the return on investment (ROI) is difficult to understand. Defense executives with military backgrounds tend to stick to the part of the process they know—their former agency. Some examples:

- Attending trade shows focused on reunions of the warfare community from which they came, such as surface navy, army aviation, carrier aviation (Tailhook), and tanks.
- Calling on former colleagues at one's former agency. Restricted communications do not encumber military officers who retire below flag rank with their former agencies.[1]
- Devoting more company time and energy to programs that benefit the service they know best—the one from which they came.

The cycle will continue like this until awareness improves. Financial performance goals often drive defense executives to focus their time on improving the business which is, they believe, within their reach. Suppose you oversee aviation programs for your company and you are a former US Air Force aviator. In that case, it makes sense to start by promoting new ideas and capabilities to the US Air Force.

The most effective defense executives learn to appreciate the rotating attention (and time) required in the 3-Ring Circus of Federal Sales^SM, Industry, Agency, and Congress. Participation in industry panels, symposia, and conferences can take significant time, depending on the executives' public positioning as thought leaders. Some invest in these activities as part of a strategic marketing and communications plan, while others must envision the return on such investment before committing.

For those with a limited understanding of how Congress works, it may be a fool's errand to devote days of travel and the associated expense to visit people on Capitol Hill. Lower levels of awareness again make this look like a lot of work for what may be a poor outcome. Those with higher levels of awareness tend to understand that one or two critical conversations can set conditions for much larger programmatic outcomes. Executives with higher levels of awareness understand that connections leading to outcomes are rarely linear. Educating decision-makers and decision participants in both the agency and Congress can be fruitful.

Case Study

As a corporate lobbyist, I oversaw interests across dozens of defense programs in Congress. One year, the Army was slow to commit to the continued funding of M-1000 trailers used to move our largest Abrams tanks from point to point. What appears to be a perpetual debate of whether we needed more tanks in this day and age was unfolding in Washington, DC. The Army Chief of Staff insisted we did not need more tanks, yet Congress sought to protect this element of industrial capacity. Congress feared if we let tank production die off, we would lose that capacity forever. My company made the M-1000 trailer in Missouri, the home state of Senator Roy Blunt, then a senior defense appropriator.

I took the sector president to meet with Senator Blunt in his office. We had a very polite 10-minute conversation describing the situation and the impact of uncertainty about tanks on revenue and jobs. The Senator agreed to look into the matter and signaled his support to maintain industrial base capacity. Within days, the Army extended the order for additional trailers. That 10-minute conversation, at the right place and time, translated to a nearly $1 billion line of revenue and the hundreds of jobs on the edge of the Ozarks it supported—time well spent.

The most sophisticated defense executives recognize that part of their time, and that of their team, needs to follow the entire budget and legislative process. Focusing on resources like time yields business intelligence along the way, reduces surprises about positioning for eventual contract opportunities, and ensures your solution, idea, or capability is fully understood. Dedication of this time and effort across the agencies and Congress is manageable by a company leader but will likely require some specific support—a lobbyist.

LOBBYING SUPPORT

In Chapter 2, I described lobbying as communicating and educating decision-makers in the executive branch and Congress. We now know there are specific rules governing the conduct of lobbying, and I've set the stage to identify how executives' higher or lower levels of process awareness can influence their decision to lobby. For those considering lobbying more formally, there are three specific ways to invest in this support.

In House

An in-house lobbyist is a full-time employee who performs the lobbying role as part of their job description, in whole or in part. As described in the rules of lobbying conduct,[2] an executive who spends less than 20% of their time on lobbying activities[3] is not required to register as a federal lobbyist. Many companies use executives hired for another purpose, such as sales, business development, general counsel, or a leadership team member as their lobbyist. An individual may have sufficient understanding, background, and communication skills to perform the lobbying role as an additional duty. If it's determined (by an internal tracking process[4]) that the individual spends more than 20% of their time on lobbying, they register per the LDA. If less, they are not required to register.

As companies reach a specific size in revenue and the number of solutions they offer the government customer, it can make financial sense to hire individuals to perform lobbying functions as their primary job. While not an exact estimate, I observe that companies with revenues from federal sales above $100 million whose executive leadership possesses sufficient process awareness see the value in hiring a full-time lobbyist as part of their staff. In academic circles, these individuals are "firm-level lobbyists."

The most successful companies with federal sales revenues above $1 billion go a step further with their federal engagement, maintaining a physical presence in Washington, DC, and creating a combined base of operation for business developers, strategists, and lobbyists. Even companies of this size that don't staff a full office will see the value of their in-house lobbyists being residents in Washington, DC. This physical presence also functions as a convenient lily pad for the senior executive team to hang their hat while conducting business in Washington, DC.

Sources of in-house lobbyists include former agency officials, former Congress and congressional staff members, former legislative liaisons for agencies, and lobbyists from other industry partners or competitors. Reputation and relationships are characteristics hiring executives tend to admire when hiring an in-house lobbyist. Some candidates bring more relevant backgrounds, expertise, and relationships than others.

An individual who worked for a very senior committee Chair must know the legislative process and have great contacts relevant to a company's interests. This highly specialized combination of experience, expertise, and relationships can be challenging to hire as pedigrees are few. As such, companies may opt for someone with less significant congressional experience, like a former staff member of a relevant personal staff. Others will value an individual with more agency experience versus congressional experience, figuring that the hire will at least understand the overall process. Finding someone with both the executive branch and congressional expertise is challenging and often requires more than one hire.

Members of Congress who leave the office with an eye toward lobbying face a mandatory two-year cooling-off period where they cannot lobby Congress. The cooling-off does not prohibit them from lobbying the executive branch or offering counsel on strategic issues for any company that hires them. Members of Congress retain special access to parts of the Capitol Hill mere mortals can never go such as congressional fitness centers, unescorted access within the actual Capitol, floor privileges in their former chamber (House or Senate), parking on Capitol Hill, and access to private House and Senate dining rooms. Former congressional staff tends to go to individual corporations after leaving the Hill, while former members see the greater financial reward of performing contract support for multiple companies.

Contract Support

"Hanging a shingle" is a common term used by individuals who work independently as independent consultants. With little more than a few minutes on Legal Zoom and payment of a state corporate filing fee, they are now entrepreneurs, presidents, and CEOs of their own "practice." I say this with malice toward none, as I ultimately chose to provide contract support to companies in need. With good reason, I'll add, as the need for such support is great.

> Get Funded—There is a higher barrier to entry for a nail technician or hair stylist than to become a lobbyist!

Independent consultants who lobby can be a cost-effective way for companies to make a limited investment in lobbying without absorbing the loaded cost of a full-time executive, often 1.5 times or more of the base salary for a junior-level executive. Contract support might specialize in a particular agency in the executive branch, committee(s) of interest in Congress, or some combination. These experts at critical processes and contract support often maintain strong relationships with process participants and decision-makers with whom they meet far more often than an executive from a single company would have occasion.

If someone hired as contract support represents multiple companies with different (non-competitive) interests, it means many more occasions to meet with relevant decision-makers over time on those multiple issues. Their relationships will be stronger on the surface and, ideally, credible. Over time, contracted support may gain a reputation as able to orchestrate meetings, introduce the capabilities of your solutions, or even influence decisions based on more thoughtful messaging.

Most contract support in the Washington, DC arena are interested in a predictable revenue stream, so they make themselves available for a recurring retainer paid monthly, quarterly, or even annually. Others may band together, forming professional partnerships; multiple individual LLCs operating under a common banner. Still, others may be associated with a law or public relations firm. The combinations are endless; some endure while others rise and fall with leadership changes in the administration and Congress. The larger the firm, the more bureaucratic tendencies it will reveal: account leads, contract terms, meeting rhythms, and varying accountabilities.

Common threads of benefits of contract support, regardless of their structures, include the following:

- They are less costly than full-time employees.
- They offer flexible terms of support in both cost and duration.
- They are more efficient by engaging at the right time and place.

By outsourcing the work associated with lobbying activities, executives maintain the freedom to focus primarily on the business of their business, remaining below the 20% threshold requiring lobbying reporting, and efficiently garner the support of decision-makers while investing less time in the effort.

There is a specific distinction regarding compensation of contract support in business development versus lobbying. Contracted business development support will offer a much lower ongoing retainer in exchange for a small percentage of the ultimate federal contract. Fractions of a percent of a multi-million-dollar contract can be rewarding for a skilled BD hand. However, the law precludes lobbyists from taking such a "success fee." Lobbyists are not eligible for compensation based on a percentage of the sale. Contract lobbyists will jointly assess the value of the hiring company's objectives against the anticipated level of effort in determining what they deem a reasonable fee.

There are norms in contract lobbying fees, yet no definitive matrix sets such fees. Jack Abramoff famously took advantage of clients by charging exorbitant fees for services; in conjunction with felonious activity to secure federal funding and policy outcomes. He was appropriately jailed and even had anti-corruption lobbying legislation[5] named in his "honor," the Justice Against Corruption on K Street Act (the JACK Act).

Coalition Lobbying

Companies within the defense industrial base often get their first exposure to lobbying through participation in supplier days or "fly-ins." Large primes hope to blanket the decision-makers with a common message told through multiple perspectives. For example, the Submarine Industrial Base Council (SIBC) has existed for over three decades. Hundreds of suppliers from across the nation come to Washington, DC, annually to tout the hometown benefits of submarine construction to their members of Congress.

Get Funded—The geographic diversity of coalitions equates to diversified political support.

Not surprisingly, the F-35 has suppliers in nearly every congressional district in the country.[6] Some companies conduct the fly-in not for one program but to demonstrate their broad reach across the entire defense industrial base. Suppliers of all programs are encouraged to tell their company's individual story but under the rubric of their contribution to the major prime. Many voices with a common message told simultaneously can demonstrate the strength of a coalition.

We often think of unions like teachers, postal workers, and airline pilots as coalitions with expansive bases of support. Similarly, the American Association of Retired Persons (AARP), the US Chamber of Commerce, and health professionals also support a common message told through potentially millions of voices. The difference is that the latter groups tend to lobby through professional messaging without bringing their entire membership to Washington, DC. Their membership rolls, letter and phone campaigns, and extensive commercial advertising amplify the organizations' messages to Washington, DC. Bringing millions of members to Washington, DC, is impractical, but the story can be more effective when professionally orchestrated.

Case Study

A company president of a valve company comes to Washington, DC, for an annual gathering of suppliers for aircraft carriers. They meet individually with the staff of members of Congress in their state. The high-level dialog goes like this:

President: Thank you for meeting with us today, and thank you and Congressman Jones for your ongoing support of defense. We're here today to express the importance of building a new aircraft carrier.

Staffer: Nice to (see/meet) you. You know Congressman Jones supports national defense and believes in a strong military but doesn't sit on a defense committee.

President: I appreciate that, and I am confident Congressman Jones knows colleagues on the committees and would benefit from knowing our perspective. We employ 475 skilled workers, and an aircraft carrier equates to about $20 million in revenue over two years.

Staffer: Yes, thanks for that clarification. How's the job market for you? Are you hiring? Do you have the skilled labor you need?

President: Well, yes and no. Having certainty in future orders helps everyone feel confident about where we are.

The message is clear. There are jobs in the district associated with a big program. The two may spend a few more minutes going back and forth. But the message was told simply and well by a company president who tried to come to Washington, DC, to convey it personally.

Third-Party Advocacy

Third-party advocacy presents support or non-support on topical issues through multiple means. Think tanks, newspaper and magazine editorials, and even professional commentators can convey a message to the public square to shape an outcome. The transactional nature of third-party advocacy is only sometimes evident on the surface and warrants at least a second glance before consuming the message.

Think tanks come in various sizes and exist to examine policies from multiple angles while proffering positions through various media such as publications, panels, symposia, and award recognition. Each has a general focus and may or may not associate loosely or closely with a political ideology. Think tanks are often staffed with full-time academic fellows or part-time associate fellows who are experts in particular disciplines within an area of expertise. In defense, there might be experts in naval warfare or aviation. Other think tanks have staff able to look across the entire national security landscape and offer commentary throughout the year.

The revenue models of think tanks vary, so one must view their materials cautiously. Long-standing charitable contributions endow some. Others sustain by subscriptions paid with corporate funds. Still, others are purely academic in nature and associated with universities. Understanding who funds a particular public position can matter greatly. Ethical standards suggest that positions are taken, like promoting more aircraft carriers, tanks, wheeled vehicles, or even a top-line budget number, would contain adequate disclosure of the interests funding the think tank. Disclosure is often opaque or difficult to discover directly.

It's common for think tanks to be staffed with former government officials, or conversely, those waiting to be tapped for a senior government position. Think tanks are not unique to national security. Still, there is enough space to learn about Washington, DC, merely by observing the behaviors of think tanks, reading their published materials, and the rotational patterns of staff who move through government and back.

There are plenty of print and digital publications across all areas of government. "Breaking Defense," "The Hill," "Bloomberg Government," "Defense One," "Inside Defense," and "Punchbowl" are just some of the more recognizable ones. These publications are staffed with journalists of varying backgrounds under continual deadlines to support an ongoing flow of breaking news, time-sensitive alerts, and daily summaries, each with attention-worthy headlines. The revenue models for each rely on subscriptions that can cost thousands of dollars per seat annually and advertising by willing participants to include companies and even programs. For example, open a web page of The Hill to read an article, and you will quickly receive screen pop-ups for various large defense companies. This concept is not unique to defense, but the biggest primes pay big for this exposure because they know decision-makers read from these sources.

Opinion pieces appear in these trade journals daily, as in *The New York Times*, *The Wall Street Journal*, or the *Los Angeles Times*. A difference is that the bar for publication in trade press is notably lower than that for national press. Opinions are commentary from various industry players such as company executives, former agency officials, and even consultants. I regularly submit commentary inputs to professional magazines, sometimes intending to shape a preferred outcome. Occasionally, a senior agency official will write something public or have a speech converted into an article. This communication typically only happens after an agency vetting process approves such publication. Some writers, who may also work in think tanks, write commentary for a fee paid by a company and fail to disclose that remuneration.

Punditry in Washington, DC, has been around for centuries, but the channels through which it conveys have grown exponentially: print, television, digital, and streaming. All pundits are telling their stories for a reason. None do it for free. Pundits are often in business for themselves, and punditry is but one revenue stream for them. This communication is within their right to speak publicly on any topic they deem themselves qualified. But the audience must know that some pundits are far less qualified, and the audience should know what other entanglements the individual has concerning the commentary offered. Like think tank disclosure, a financial linkage is often not evident to the consumer of the information. It takes considerable time to be ready to offer commentary on breaking news. Why do they do it? It's good for their business.

POLITICAL GIVING

This section of the book might make you feel like you are about to touch a live wire. It shouldn't and I'll "ground you" on a few of the basics so you can be more conversant in concepts of political giving and the bogeyman of "money in politics." There is an area of federal law called campaign finance law or election law. There are troves of academic studies and examinations of this area of law at all levels, including rulings by the US Supreme Court.

While a campaign contribution can express free speech and support of a candidate, that support is also an investment. This section won't make you an expert in federal campaign finance. Instead, I only want to frame it into your field of view and explain how others around you may use political giving to their advantage. Know these three rules, and you will be ahead of more than 90% of your competitors:

1. *Running for election costs money.* Messaging and travel are the big-ticket costs of an election campaign, and some districts and states are more challenging than others. The state of Florida has 27 congressional districts; Wyoming has two. The media markets for each state are entirely different, as are their costs. Similarly, contrast the many congressional districts surrounding Los Angeles and Chicago, again with multiple and overlapping media markets. Reaching potential voters costs money.
2. *Campaign contributions are a form of free speech.* It is your right to give money to a political campaign.[7] I'll explain how this occurs through different channels below but know that you may give individually or, in some cases, make corporate contributions to political entities.
3. *Political giving is not required to achieve outcomes in Washington, DC.* Further, the timing of a contribution with an expectation of an outcome is expressly illegal—the notorious "pay to play" or "quid pro quo."

Remember these three underlying rules, and you'll be able to identify where political giving *might* make sense in your overall communications strategy and how to avoid making a mistake that one could interpret as wrongdoing. Leave the most profound details and nuance of political giving to the fundraising professionals of the political class. Consider this the crib sheet for executives.

Personal Contributions

Individuals may contribute a specified amount to federal election campaigns for each separate election. Your Senators and representatives run for office every six years or every two years, respectively. For most, there is a primary and a general election. That's two elections to which you may contribute during the period of the election cycle. In 2023, the individual contribution limit *per election* is $2900. That means you could contribute $2900 to the primary and another $2900 to the general election of any candidate or each of multiple candidates. $5800 is a lot of money.

Typically, a candidate will host fundraising events like receptions and dinners where you might contribute a portion of that $5800 to a specific event. You may know you plan to contribute $5800 eventually, so you can choose to do it at once and then be invited to all of the events in the coming election cycle. That equates to face-time and a short conversation with the Representative or Senator. During such conversations, you express support for the member or you might even discuss what's important to you and your business.

Contributing individually to individual campaigns is costly. While it's true members of Congress need to raise money for re-election, this part of the process can be a filter that keeps people away. It does so for two reasons: people need to understand the rules, or they need discretionary funds to contribute.

Political Action Committees (PACs)

A PAC is a legal entity whereby people with common interests pool their money for eventual distribution to candidates. You likely belong to associations that contribute a portion of your dues to PACs, such as AARP, realtors, teachers, and farmers. Companies are allowed to form PACs and solicit contributions from management class employees. These smaller contributions are deducted from paychecks and automatically placed in the PAC accounts. The individual limit to contribute to a PAC in 2023 is $5000 over a year.

A board governs PACs and by-laws specific to each PAC specify the PAC board membership and conduct. The board decides to which candidates PAC funds will disburse. A defense company PAC will typically support members of committees of interest, members surrounding company facilities, and members who generally promote national security. The theory of PACs is that one's individual contributions, when pooled, can support many more candidates than the individual might be able to support alone. "Your PAC contribution goes further than your individual contribution" is a common refrain of a PAC manager.

The largest defense PACs collect contributions from thousands of employees and maintain more than $1 million in cash on hand. Just using round numbers, a PAC with one hundred $1,000 contributions can support ten candidates at the maximum allowable level ($5,000 per election). You can see that the very large companies with very large PACs can support more candidates than a smaller company with a smaller PAC.

A small business could form its own PAC comprised of its leaders if they were to register with the Federal Election Commission (FEC) as a PAC. This could allow multiple executives to pool their contributions in a PAC for subsequent distribution as the PAC board determines. Again, this way the contribution goes to more candidates than the individual might otherwise afford alone.

Party-Affiliated Campaign Committees (RNC/ RNCC/RNSC/DNC/DCCC/DNSC)

Each of the major political parties has their own "committee" focused on elections: Republican National Committee, Democratic National Committee, and so on for the House and Senate as well. Each of these committees also functions as a PAC with specified contribution limits for each. The amounts vary depending on support of a presidential election, an inauguration, or a standard election for a congressional term. Those additional PACs reflect additional opportunities for political giving.

It Just Is

One can argue the merits or unfairness of political giving. The rules governing campaign contributions are set in law by Congress, in policy by the Federal Election Commission (FEC), and ultimately enforced in the judicial system. Political fundraising is a cottage industry staffed by extraordinarily skilled technologists. Email, social media, television, and digital streaming services offer more ways than ever for a fundraiser to get directly to you with their solicitation.

Congress is fully aware of how this works even as they rail against it during public debate, and their fundraising team simultaneously solicits contributions during the same debate. I'm not here to condone the merits or argue for change. I want you to understand it is present, and you have an opportunity to participate. It's for you to determine if it makes sense as an investment in support of your overall sales strategy. A former Captain of mine who later became an admiral described the state of affairs accurately, "it just is."

Many have determined that it makes sense. Nearly all top-performing federal contractors have a PAC. Unfortunately, the overwhelming majority of company executives in the industrial base do not know the information I just conveyed. As I'll describe in Chapter 7 on compliance, few executives understand these rules and the associated state of play.

Return on Investment (ROI)

Each of the investments described in this chapter comes with a cost of time, talent, and treasure. They require choices and tradeoffs. Executives faced with limited resources need a sense of certainty about the ROI. A leader asks myriad questions when evaluating investments, but, with respect to support of the sales effort, might ask:

- How much staff can one afford?
- Should we augment staff with specialized contracted support?
- Who can best help us shape a message? And where?
- Can company leadership be a thought leader in any of the public fora?
- If we pay for third-party advocacy, will others know it was us?
- What audience are we trying to specifically reach?

- Should I make campaign contributions?
- Can I encourage my staff to make contributions?
- Is the investment worthwhile?

In my research, defense executives were acutely aware of returns when commenting on investment. A manufacturing vice president stated,

> Well, I know what we paid for our lobbyist every year. Did that pay for itself. I would say in our specific instance at [redacted for masking], I think it was very, very helpful. He's a very good lobbyist. He had a lot of credibility with the staff. He could get in and to see a lot of the Congressmen. He spoke with a lot of authority.

The same executive, whose company previously used contracted lobbying support, continued when describing the calculation,

> I think we would be encouraged if we saw a more favorable business environment that we could affect through legislation. If we could affect a more favorable business environment. If we thought there was a chance to get that kind of outcome or effect, that would definitely motivate us to get more actively involved in the legislative process.

One president of a small business saw value in communicating with Congress beyond the ability to shape an outcome. The return could take the form of improving reputation or awareness of the company's presence and impact. Commenting on the value of being known by one's member of Congress, he said,

> I think it's a matter as I look at it's ensuring that your elected representatives, understand what you do as a company and the value that you provide that community, whether it's in revenue that's brought in to the community and in community service that you do as a company.

As large as an industry like defense appears, the number of lobbyists registered to represent defense interests is less than 1,000 of just over 12,000 federally registered lobbyists. That's right, the largest portion of the discretionary budget (defense is $850 billion in the fiscal year 2023) is lobbied by fewer than one-tenth of the lobbying community. More surprisingly, defense is not in the top ten industries as measured by lobbying spending. Pharma, agriculture, and insurance, for example, have far more lobbyists, and those industries spend more on lobbying than the defense industry (defense is not in the top ten). Why is that?

It has much to do with the policies associated with those other industries. Policies that touch the lives of citizens require highly sophisticated messaging that takes place not only in Washington, DC, but countless media markets throughout the country. Broad-based messaging can be expensive when trying to move public opinion on complex policies.

> Get Funded—Who among us actually understands their insurance company's periodic explanation of benefits?

But what the most successful defense companies recognize is that when their message can be told well, consistently, and to the right levels of decision maker across the agency and Congress, those same companies prefer to participate in the process. They see a return, or they would not make the effort.

SUMMARY

Multiple investment decisions are associated with the federal sale, and investment is a zero-sum game. All executives face the challenge of the stewardship of finite resources. I've acknowledged some areas where particular attention might help you begin to shape outcomes earlier in the process. Time management, business development, communication, lobbying, and political giving can support the influence of decision-makers on your sale—before the contracting process ever starts.

It's for you to evaluate better how you've distributed your investment. Your self-assessed experience may be proving inadequate to the task. In Chapter 6, I'll identify how expertise further differentiates winners from losers in federal sales.

NOTES

1. Individuals involved in acquisition decisions are subject to different criteria in their post-military careers. Some acquisition officials face a lifetime ban from engaging in issues on which they once decided contracts and terms. More senior officers are subject to a 1-year or 2-year "cooling off" period before re-engaging their former agency directly on a business matter.

2. See https://lda.senate.gov/system/public/.

3. See https://www.senate.gov/legislative/Lobbying/Lobby_Disclosure_Act/3_Definitions.htm.

4. There is no specific tracking system required, only that a company has some system in place.

5. https://www.congress.gov/bill/115th-congress/house-bill/7104/all-info.

6. See https://www.lockheedmartin.com/f35/news-and-features/everything-you-need-to-know-about-the-f-35c.html, Lockheed Martin leads the F-35 industry team with Northrop Grumman, BAE Systems and Pratt & Whitney. The program is managed by the Department of Defense's F-35 Joint Program Office. More than 1,900 suppliers build and sustain the F-35 program in 48 U.S. states and in more than 10 countries.

7. All political campaign contributions above $200 are recorded by the Federal Election Commission and maintained in a publicly searchable data base at www.fec.gov.

6

Experience or Expertise: Time vs. Competence

Defense executives overwhelmingly credit on-the-job training (OJT) as the crucible one must endure succeeding in the defense business—one must learn by doing. But spending "20 years in the Army before this job (selling in defense)" doesn't translate to 20-plus years of expertise. Instead, it's just time on station. Experience and expertise are not synonyms, though they are often used interchangeably and, therefore, incorrectly.

> Get Funded—Experience is personally observing or encountering something over time. Expertise is expert skill or knowledge; expertness.

Filling gaps in their knowledge, defense executives often turn to people they know and trust from within their network when faced with ambiguity while performing their current business development, sales, or other executive roles. OJT can work, but the lack of standardized performance measures means that the company is paying the School of Hard Knocks tuition. Where does one turn to learn their role?

THE CURSE OF ON-THE-JOB TRAINING (OJT)

Understanding how to do one's job seems an obvious requirement for any successful executive. Defense executives ascend to leadership roles through

DOI: 10.4324/9781003454885-6

two primary paths, prior military service, or from within the defense industry through a traditional track such as engineering, operations, or business development. Each path produces extraordinarily knowledgeable senior executives with very different business DNA.

Those who served in uniform believe they understand the customer and its culture because they've "been there and done that," "got the t-shirt (for deployment(s))," or otherwise participated in operations one only sees while on active duty. Those who come up through the more traditional business track and did not serve on active duty also believe they understand their business and customer because they've been working in the industry for years, if not for decades. Depending on the company culture, tensions can simmer between those who served on active duty and those who did not. Which path is better is a pointless debate; the underlying issue is many executives of both tracks arrive in position with a weak understanding of the integrated federal budgeting, funding, and acquisition processes regardless of their upbringing. This phenomenon is evident because it's impossible to become an expert in all phases of the inter-connected federal processes while simultaneously performing one's day job.

I interviewed executives of both pedigrees in my research. Regardless of how they came into position, the majority struggle to convey true depth of knowledge regarding the federal process. Where does one turn to learn the processes described until now: budgeting, legislation, acquisition, and contracting? Any of these four major processes are worthy of their coursework and certification. Degree programs for parts of the process are emerging at major universities in the Washington, DC area, and some research participants acknowledge attending some specialized training over time.

Over the preceding decades, significant elements of acquisition reforms focus on providing coursework and certifications—primarily for the government buyers. The Defense Acquisition University (DAU) exists to support a professional acquisition workforce—of government employees! Although some civilians can access portions of this training, it's only in minimal form. Participation at DAU by industry requires a "seat" be available and that the executive can be away from their primary business role for the duration of the course.

Degree and certification programs are available to learn about budgeting, federal comptrollership, and even Congress and the legislative process. Universities in the Washington, DC area also offer recurring programs that get at parts of these processes. Courses on budgeting and congressional procedure are generally not top of mind for a defense executive. The zero-sum nature of investment in Chapter 5 reinforces the challenge of approving an executive's expense for this additional training.

I've previously described a cottage industry surrounding GOVCON. Countless short courses and seminars are available throughout the country under the auspices of the Small Business Association (SBA) or industry trade groups such as the National Defense Industrial Association (NDIA). The ubiquity of such programs reinforces the perception that the contract phase is the entry point of the federal buying process. These programs tend to focus on contracting.

So where do defense executives turn? One research participant, a vice president, identified his experiences as "a combination of classroom training opportunities from how Washington works and resourcing 101 courses...week long, in-house training on federal budgets and how the money flows and things like that."

One vice president and formal naval officer acknowledged, "No, I have had no formal training," while a vice president with ten years in his present role recounted, "I guess I learned, through some very, very painful experiences."

Yet another vice president, with less than ten years in the defense industry and six in his current role, acknowledged, "So [I] probably learned most of what I apply in my daily routine now from working with some of those other companies post-active duty." All participants in my research admit that OJT was their primary source of learning how to perform their part of the complex process.

Lobbyists tend to follow a similar methodology of learning through OJT. Whether a former member of Congress, a former congressional staff member, or a former "senior government official" of the executive branch, the pattern of learning by doing is often the same for those who become professional lobbyists in any capacity: in-house, contracted support, or third-party advocate representing an association or coalition.

Efforts to self-govern the lobbying profession by developing training and certification programs have failed. The American League of Lobbyists (ALL), renamed as the Association of Government Relations Professionals (AGRP), survived for decades before ultimately folding. Today, the National Institute of Lobbying and Ethics (NILE) and the Government Relations Association (GRA) serve as industry associations for the profession. Each offers classes and seminars; however, they tend to draw participants already resident in the Washington, DC area.

Alas, there is no course or credential required of lobbying. To lobby at the federal level, one must register per the LDA. To be hired as a lobbyist, one must demonstrate a capacity to perform the expected role of a lobbyist in educating decision-makers, moving information effectively within the government processes, and ultimately shaping outcomes. Most lobbyists come to the profession after serving in or around the federal government and Congress. Landing a role as a lobbyist in any capacity is based on a combination of prior service in the legislative or executive branch, demonstrable skills of communication and influence, and an ability to connect and network effectively.

Networks and Mentors

It's human nature to want to look our best and present ourselves as doing our best. One needs to look no further than social media to see how professionals present themselves, their companies, and their successes. We tend only to reveal our best selves to the general public. But executives rely on their networks when searching for answers and navigating uncertain environments. In my research and advisory work, executives acknowledge turning to those they know and trust when searching for answers or revealing their professional shortcomings.

Get Funded—When is the last time you saw a post on LinkedIn highlighting a corporate failure in which the individual posting played a prominent role?

When exploring the sources of mentors that a post-military defense executive seeks, I find they call on former leaders who have transitioned into industry. Although this may appear a prominent place to turn for counsel, more than this resource is needed. Most military people feel they have diverse networks stemming from their multiple duty stations, global travel, and time spent growing a network during their active-duty years. In reality, those sometimes geographically diverse networks need to be more comprehensive in the type of technical expertise available to draw from. A former uniformed US Air Force acquisition official, one research participant, self-assessed his ability to blend OJT with mentorship: "25 years of watching other people ahead of me in the chain. Truly the school of hard knocks, and being brought along by a variety of mentors along the way."

Several of the companies I work with form additional advisory boards to support the corporate leadership team. Advisory boards are separate and distinct from the legal governance and fiduciary responsibilities accompanying a corporate board. I see advisory boards used more often by companies led by business leaders who did not previously serve in the military. Whether the position is full-time, in-house, contracted support, or volunteer, studies show that a majority of senior military (flag and general) officers find post-active-duty work in the defense industry.

Business leaders who ascend through traditional business disciplines appear to recognize that they do not know it all and seek ways to fill those gaps in their knowledge. Their business networks are diverse, and their advisory board members bring specific Washington, DC backgrounds. The advisors have "been there, done that," while serving in very unique positions.

In some cases, advisory board members receive a notional stipend, or at least have their board-related expenses covered. They want to share their expertise and are not necessarily so transactional about the exchange. It's common to see retired admirals, generals, and members of the senior executive service (SES) serve on advisory boards. Advisory board members are willing to share their critical perspectives drawn from activities the business executive would likely never have faced: testifying before a congressional hearing, balancing readiness trade-offs with future investment, interacting with very senior US and foreign government officials, or even briefing at the National Security Council. Recognizing how to bring this diversity into corporate executives' decision models differentiates the best companies over time.

Former members of Congress and former congressional staff who transition to lobbying after their time on Capitol Hill similarly check in with former colleagues who have gone before them and are working in industry. Most who come from a position on Capitol Hill have quietly collected an expansive Rolodex of industry contacts (and industry lobbyists) who visited them while in Congress with a legitimate business. Informational meetings where one might test the market for a post-Hill job opportunity occur routinely. It's perfectly legal and not unlike professional networking that takes place in other industries.

The concept of networking and reaching out to mentors is the same as any other industry. My observation in the defense industry is that these connections form a primary path to initial and subsequent industry positions for those with ambition to move up and those who seek the perceived relative safety of a corporate position. Not unlike someone with experience on Wall Street might change positions while maintaining proximity to New York City's financial district, so to do those with specific Washington, DC experience.

"I KNOW A GUY"

Knowing where to turn to fill gaps in one's knowledge requires a degree of humility, and an ability and willingness to communicate a shortcoming or need (the gaps). Further, one requires access to someone who either knows someone, or knows someone who knows someone. "Knowing a guy," to paraphrase from the television series *Breaking Bad* loosely, can be helpful in better learning essential federal process as well as in gaining access to decision-makers.

While Washington, DC is a relatively small city when compared to most capitals, within industries servicing the federal customer, Washington, DC can also evoke a small town. It's sometimes said of those in the defense industry, "look around because you'll be seeing these same people in different positions for the next 25 years" (Figure 6.1).

In my research, a CEO of a technology start-up, who had also served in US Air Force acquisition, acknowledged learning about how to bring in advisors who understood into his team. His honesty is evident when responding to how he learned to become more expert on both lobbying and advisement,

> Interestingly, learning about how to work with the lobbying industry requires you to then learn how to work with the advisory industry. Which is an entire other set of people who don't do lobbying for you, but they're strategic business advisors, corporate advisors who help you with business strategy. They often know the appropriate lobbying strategy and

FIGURE 6.1
Your narrow networks.

can put you in contact with the lobbying firms. I don't think lobbying is one of those skill sets you learn from watching YouTube videos and go to courses. It is so personal and it is so opaque that it's one of the things you kind of have to get on the inside and start doing it to understand how it really works.

Another senior executive, a retired two-star admiral working for a defense solutions provider, echoed the recognition that seeking specialized support is a part of his company's strategy:

We would hire someone who knows how to do that. We're not a big enough company to have a full-time employee, at least initially. That's how we typically do things when we get into something new is we'll hire a consultant to advise us on the best way to make an approach.

Another retired US Navy officer now working as a business developer captured the challenge of "finding the right person in the system to get to talk to because it's such a mammoth structure, drilling down and finding that right person is half the battle," when clarifying his understanding of knowing how to network and connect.

In my research, some responses to the question of where one turns to learn more about lobbying and interacting with agencies and Congress included the following:

"Mentors along the way,"
"[Knowing to] hire someone who knows how to do that,"
"[I would] go ask some people,"
"Building relationships in anything in life is the most
  important thing."

Evaluating available support in Washington, DC relies overwhelmingly on word of mouth—referrals. Knowing people who understand how things work, with whom to speak or when and where to ask for a favor or connection to a decision maker requires connections. To the companies with team members or "Washington Ops" teams resident inside the beltway, this can seem an obviosity.

But what about for the hundreds of thousands of companies that don't have exposure to Washington, DC decision making? They have no idea with whom to speak because they often aren't even aware there are conversations to be had.

Get Funded—It's not different than tennis legend Serena Williams showing up to play on the LPGA. Wrong sport, wrong preparation, and sub-optimal outcome.

WHO'S ON YOUR TEAM?

One needs to only look at the makeup of the various Washington, DC offices of companies across all industries to see the array of specific expertise resident or on contract with each office. Companies committed to working the entire process use specialized support to their advantage. Those companies recognize the potential for improved outcomes by investing in hiring those with expertise.

The largest companies maintain Washington, DC offices with dozens or hundreds of specialists across government relations, staff, and operations functions. Lobbyists, business developers, strategists, external communications connectors, public relations, contracting, and marketing to name a few. They may not all need to be resident in Washington, DC. Still, the learning point is that they are highly specialized to represent their company to these required federal functions associated with the federal sale. Companies without representation in Washington, DC are simply not fully participating in the sales process.

In 2009, a stir[1] swept across the defense landscape when the Department of Defense hired back retired flag and general officers as advisors and trainers at double their active-duty salaries. It's a Catch-22 in that the DoD must draw on the expertise its senior officials garnered to train the most senior officers. Such expertise cannot be found on the open market with a hiring firm as one might find a proven CFO or COO with transportation experience for example.

Former civilian government officials are similarly available to the industries they formerly regulated or supported, such as health care, insurance, or finance. As with former defense officials, the pool of eligible support to bring in-house or hire as a contractor can be relatively small within the specific industry. Referrals, networking, reputation, and, yes, "knowing a guy" is often how the connections to this talent get made.

The learning point is to recognize that building your team that takes you to the federal market requires experience, expertise, a timely and relevant network, proximity to the decision-makers, and a degree of humility to acknowledge where your team needs more specific support. Such acknowledgment requires that even the very best leaders allow themselves to be appropriately vulnerable when attempting to match talent to need.

SUMMARY

Throughout Chapter 6, I've identified ways companies must supplement their talents to succeed with federal sales. Those companies with direct exposure to the Washington, DC environment better recognize how small their industry can appear in the eyes of the federal buyer, federal regulator, or congressional oversight committees. Access to the requisite expertise requires knowledge of where experts may reside and how they integrate into your team and are effectively deployed.

Incorporating this talent requires understanding the law and policy governing communications with Congress, government agencies, and federal buyers. In Chapter 7, I'll identify some rules and rules of thumb that will lead you to better decisions using the expertise you bring to your team.

NOTE

1 See one report here, https://abcnews.go.com/Politics/retired-military-officers-retire-paid-consultants/story?id=9115368.

7

Lobbying Compliance

Ask any defense executive about their company's adherence to lobbying laws and rules. The odds are that you'll get a response related to ethics, campaign contributions, or for a dynamic company, maybe what is allowed during a congressman's visit to the plant. "General counsel handles that," "I give to the PAC (political action committee)," and "we get approval to support industry days on the Hill" are common refrains.

Similarly, ask a former government official about the rules governing their ability to communicate with their former executive branch agency or Congress. You'll hear some reference to a wait period, a cooling off period, being radioactive for a while, 20% of their time, or a direct denial of their fundamental role, "no, I don't lobby." Each response has some trace evidence of facts or the individual receiving an annual PowerPoint training brief. But very few who do not lobby can articulate the compliance issues of lobbying government. There's that lack of awareness peeking through—but can we see it in ourselves?

Some law firms focus on political law whose lawyers can readily interpret the law and policy of government relations. The very best companies that dedicate resources to influence in Washington, DC all have outside counsel on call to assist with interpretation of compliance issues that accompany the influence. Unfortunately, the very best companies are also in the minority. Just as only a fraction of a percent of companies use lobbyists, a similarly tiny fraction even tries to understand the governing law and policy better. It doesn't look very easy, so it gets ignored. That ignorance contributes to less effective outcomes, and the cycle continues.

DOI: 10.4324/9781003454885-7

My legal disclaimer: I am not an attorney, don't play one on TV, and did not sleep at a Holiday Inn last night. I aim to identify some areas where you must have conversational knowledge to the degree that you can recognize when you should seek professional help with your federal communications.

THE LAW

In Chapter 2, I identified that the Lobbying Disclosure Act (LDA) governs lobbying activities and provides definitions to clarify the participants and the acts associated with lobbying. Review of the law can provide practical annual training to leadership teams if for no other reason than to periodically revisit the discussion of the teams' talent distribution in this area. I'll quote some relevant definitions[1] of which any senior executive selling to the federal government should be aware. After listing these key definitions, I'll briefly identify how the LDA fits with policies of which executives should similarly be aware.

Lobbying Activities—The term "lobbying activities" means lobbying contacts and efforts in support of such contacts, including preparation and planning activities, research, and other background work that is intended, at the time it is performed, for use in contacts, and coordination with the lobbying activities of others.

Lobbying Contact—The term "lobbying contact" means any oral or written communication (including an electronic communication) to a covered executive branch official or a covered legislative branch official that is made on behalf of a client with regard to—

i. the formulation, modification, or adoption of Federal legislation (including legislative proposals);
ii. the formulation, modification, or adoption of a Federal rule, regulation, Executive order, or any other program, policy, or position of the United States Government;
iii. the administration or execution of a Federal program or policy (including the negotiation, award, or administration of a Federal contract, grant, loan, permit, or license); or

iv. the nomination or confirmation of a person for a position subject to confirmation by the Senate.

Covered Executive Branch Official—The term "covered executive branch official" means—

A. the President;
B. the Vice President;
C. any officer or employee, or any other individual functioning in the capacity of such an officer or employee, in the Executive Office of the President;
D. any officer or employee serving in a position in level I, II, III, IV, or V of the Executive Schedule, as designated by statute or Executive order;
E. any member of the uniformed services whose pay grade is at or above O–7 under section 201 of title 37, United States Code; and
F. any officer or employee serving in a position of a confidential, policy-determining, policy-making, or policy-advocating character described in section 7511(b)(2)(B) of title 5, United States Code.

Covered Legislative Branch Official—The term "covered legislative branch official" means—

A. a member of Congress;
B. an elected officer of either House of Congress;
C. any employee of, or any other individual functioning in the capacity of an employee of—
   i.   a member of Congress;
   ii. a committee of either House of Congress;
   iii. the leadership staff of the House of Representatives or the leadership staff of the Senate;
   iv. a joint committee of Congress; and
   v.   a working group or caucus organized to provide legislative services or other assistance to members of Congress; and
D. any other legislative branch employee serving in a position described under section 109(13) of the Ethics in Government Act of 1978 (5 U.S.C. App.).

Lobbyist—The term "lobbyist" means any individual who is employed or retained by a client for financial or other compensation for services that include more than one lobbying contact, other than an individual whose lobbying activities constitute less than 20% of the time engaged in the services provided by such an individual to that client over a three-month period.

Piecing the definitions together, an executive can see that they or their employees may be lobbying, but not calling it lobbying and therefore not reporting it as lobbying. Lobbying contact of a defined covered official in the executive branch or Congress is lobbying by someone fitting the definition of a lobbyist. It may also be consulting, advising, business development, networking, and even socializing, but it can also be lobbying. Suppose one were to try and demure that the contact was about a long-standing friendship or other form of innocent communication. In that case, there are various tests within the law to precisely confirm what is an act of lobbying.

Remember the shadow lobbyist described in Chapter 2? Shadow lobbyists fail to report their activities for one of two reasons: ignorance of the law, or a belief that the law does not apply to them and that nobody is paying that close of attention. Regardless of the reason, it can be a point of significant exposure for a company as I'll describe how the LDA is put to practice by policy and how financial liability for the failure to comply with the LDA is penalized.

The Policy

Amendments to the LDA, codified in the 2007 Honest Leadership and Open Government Act (HLOGA), spell out more precise rules to govern ethical behaviors of members of Congress as well as lobbyists. Members of Congress and executive branch personnel of particular seniorities must abide by the post-employment restrictions of HLOGA.

Cooling off periods are when members of Congress must wait after leaving office before lobbying any part of the legislative branch; Representatives must wait one year, and Senators must wait two years. Of interest, no such cooling off applies to legislative staffs. It's common to see senior legislative staff leaving Congress and moving directly into a corporate or contract lobbying role. The largest defense prime contractors all employ former senior congressional staff—they are current, expert, and unencumbered.

In the executive branch cooling off periods also apply to senior officials, uniformed and civilian. Still, the limitation period is one year and applies only to the agency they came from. A retired Navy Admiral could lobby the Army or Congress assuming that no complicating joint service duty is involved. Similarly, a former member of Congress or Senator could lobby the executive branch, just not Congress.

Get Funded—There was once a book titled "The Almanac of the Unelected" that identified the backgrounds of individuals in staff roles who rise in seniority and come to exert a significant influence without being elected.

Gift exchanges are forbidden with the minor exceptions too challenging to make worthwhile. Gift exchange rules apply in both directions: lobbyists may not gift senior executive branch officials or any member of Congress. Conversely, those same officials and members of Congress must refrain from soliciting a gift. There was a time when lunches, dinners, coffees, and office holiday gifts were appropriate and allowable. HLOGA drew clear lines around gift giving and set the stage for the comical yet memorable "toothpick test" of passed hors d' oeuvres being allowable in certain reception situations (Figure 7.1).

FIGURE 7.1
The "toothpick test."

Annually, the General Accountability Office (GAO) conducts a random review of lobbying compliance reports required of the LDA. The GAO regularly finds compliance among lobbyists who file reports reflecting the nature of a client relationship and the topic(s) lobbied is high. This shouldn't come as a surprise as the advertised fine for failing to comply can be $200,000 per instance of failure. Lobbying compliance among registered lobbyists remains above 90% since GAO began this annual review. The remaining 10% are mainly administrative issues.

What the GAO does not, and perhaps can't capture, is the failure to report lobbying by those not registered to lobby. The revolving door regularly services those who leave government, want to be of further service, and believe their focus on consulting and advisement exempts them from lobbying rules.

> Get Funded—While on active duty, I served with a senior Navy Captain who explained that "the law is the law, and can't be broken; but we can bend policy like a horseshoe."

BENDING THE HORSESHOE

Policy is defined[2] as "a course or principle of action by a government." Policies can derive from the law or agency level from the authorities inherent in government agencies. I've reiterated the definitions provided in lobbying law. The laws' interpretation falls to individuals following guidance provided by agencies in the executive branch or by designated officials of the legislative branch, such as the Secretary of the Senate,[3] Clerk of the House,[4] or House[5] or Senate Sergeant at Arms.[6]

SUMMARY

Chapter 7 provides legal definitions, policy interpretations, and practical applications of communications known colloquially as government relations. The most sophisticated companies that effectively sequence their communications across government while leveraging timing and relationships use lobbying as a tool. They understand the rules at least well enough to not draw unwanted attention while simultaneously shaping the acquisition playing field to their best advantage. In Chapter 8, I'll identify how the size and type of business can fuel creativity and cloud the outcomes an executive might imagine.

NOTES

1 Definitions are quoted directly from the 1995 Lobbying Disclosure Act (LDA), found here: https://www.senate.gov/legislative/Lobbying/Lobby_Disclosure_Act/3_Definitions.htm.
2 See Google's Oxford Languages.
3 See https://www.senate.gov/reference/office/secretary_of_senate.htm.
4 See https://clerk.house.gov.
5 See https://www.house.gov/the-house-explained/officers-and-organizations/sergeant-at-arm.
6 See https://www.senate.gov/reference/office/sergeant_at_arms.htm.

8

Size and Type of Business

Size matters. Or does it? Conventional wisdom would suggest that the most prominent companies have all the advantages. They have enormous budgets for people, travel, campaign contributions, public opinion writers, and stables of consultants. They can pay premium prices and buy relationships by hiring insiders passing through the revolving door. In practice, it only sometimes works that way though.

More often, what drives a company to engage in a federal opportunity is the belief that they can solve a problem with their solution. Some companies see the contours of the federal playing field differently than others. But what are those contours and, who can even see them? As is often the case, what you see depends. But depends on what?

> Get Funded—"What you see and hear depends a good deal on where you are standing." C.S. Lewis

The competitive federal opportunity unfolds over time and within the constraints of specific budget categories. We want to think that contract opportunities are open to all qualified competitors and subsequently distributed relatively to the competitive winners. They mostly are. Yet research shows that companies that participate in the legislative process, which takes place before the acquisition phase ever begins, tend to benefit from more favorable contract outcomes.[1]

Large products and platforms such as ships, aircraft, and submarines are acquired and placed on contract with funds that carry multi-year authority for the obligation. Services and commodities, on the other hand, such as office supplies, facility security, sanitation removal, and fuel

DOI: 10.4324/9781003454885-8

provisioning, must be obligated in the fiscal year for which Congress approves them with either operations and maintenance or sustainment funds. This fundamental difference in the horizon of the "life" of the funding, spanning one to seven years, inhibits or facilitates executives' imaginations of how lobbying Congress can help or hinder. Executives who can see a sufficient time horizon to position funding or adjust a policy will be more inclined to make investments in support of a more comprehensive approach to the federal sale.

> Get Funded—"Colors of Money"—A term of art in government referring to the fund's account: research and development, procurement, or operations and maintenance, for example. Colors of money are not interchangeable, and each has a specific lifespan.

Although large companies are often perceived to have traditional size advantages, such as staffing, resources, and investment reserves, that allow them to play a more robust, and sometimes careless, game in federal sales, the budget process and ability to lobby Congress make no distinctions about company size. The federal budgeting and buying process is the same for all companies, regardless of size or type. The 3-person "pre-revenue" start-up, $500 million-dollar mid-size, and multi-billion-dollar large company are all subject to the budget and funding decisions of the same complex processes. Companies of any size and type have the same access opportunity. In this chapter, I'll dispel the myth that size matters and is more a perceived element of successful federal sales than a determining factor.

HOW DO WE MEASURE SIZE?

The Small Business Administration (SBA) identifies companies by size according to their specific North American Industry Classification System (NAICS) code, using either head count or revenue as the metric. In rough terms, a head count below 500 and revenue below $41.5 million qualifies a defense company as a small business. A company can be considered small for one NAICS code, but not another. Companies designated as a small business may qualify for additional set-asides, contracts intended to support specific categories of company identified by Congress as protected.

The Addiction and Myth of Set-Asides

The Small Business Act is a federal law dating back to the late 1950s, and since its enactment, Congress regularly amends the law. Its most recent amended version[2] in the 117th Congress (2022) clarifies,

> ... the Government should aid, counsel, assist, and protect, insofar as is possible, the interests of small-business concerns in order to preserve free competitive enterprise, to insure that a fair proportion of the total purchases and contracts or subcontracts for property and services for the Government (including but not limited to contracts or subcontracts for maintenance, repair, and construction) be placed with small-business enterprises, to ensure that a fair proportion of the total sales of Government property be made to such enterprises, and to maintain and strengthen the overall economy of the Nation.

By law, as much as 25% of federal contracts are to be awarded to small business. The 25% set-asides are further divided by "socio-economic[3]" categories of small business which include women-owned, 8(a) disadvantaged, historically underutilized business (HUB) zone, and service-disabled veteran-owned. The law is well intended and grounded in substantial research confirming that innovation and economic growth in the United States overwhelmingly emanates from small businesses. The set-asides, however, acknowledge that access to capital for the set-aside categories is such that exceptional support for small business access to competitive federal opportunities requires some level of assistance.

THE ADDICTION

Companies participating in federal sales recognize the power and advantage of their access to unique set-aside programs. We look at competition for contracts through the lens of individual programs or contract opportunities. Few recognize how challenging the odds are when looking at how contracts ultimately distribute across the industrial base. The distribution of opportunity across all companies looks something like this:

- 50% of the defense acquisition dollars go to 40 companies[4] and their subs
- 25% of the acquisition dollars go to small business, which translates to about 60,000 companies
- 25% of the acquisition dollars go to everyone else, for which about 350,000 companies may compete[5]

When small businesses recognize that the competitive pool is so much smaller, 60,000 companies versus 350,000 companies, it's not difficult to see that one's overall odds of winning improve when designated as a small business. When taken down to the level of individual competitive opportunities, only a handful of small businesses may have the capacity to deliver on a specific small business set-aside, so the odds of winning a competition for a contract improve even further. In rare cases only one or two companies are qualified to deliver on a contract opportunity, offering one in two odds!

Plenty of small businesses lead with their special status when introducing themselves. "I'm a service-disabled, veteran-owned small business. We make sprockets." Similarly, "I'm an 8(a) business with our main facility in a HUB zone." The designation is secondary to the capability or capacity of the company, yet many small business owners lead with this credential in an introduction. A culture, embedded in a subset of the industrial base, conforms to staying designated as a small business. This may allow the company to sustain at an acceptable size and level of profitability such that their outgrowing such designation is not attractive to them.

Tax rates, burdens of employee health care costs, and a more intense competitive landscape can encourage small businesses to remain small. Why jump into the shark tank when one can play in the pool with a lifeguard and designated swim lanes? My unscientific observation is that those small companies whose leaders harbor big-company aspirations are in the minority. Too many small businesses are content to grow just big enough as not to outgrow their small business credential. Too many approach the small business ceiling with trepidation as opposed to vigor. Sometimes these small businesses with no eye toward growth are seen as lifestyle businesses that allow for a high-quality lifestyle for the owners.

THE MYTH

Not all small business set-asides are implemented with the purity of the law's intent, to give small business a lift in a capital-challenged environment. Small businesses can make desirable partners to large companies because of the small business' eligibility for set-aside contracts. Partnering between small and large businesses can represent the best of both worlds. A partnership or prime/sub-prime relationship allows a large company to access the small business opportunity by subcontracting to the small business. The small business gains the benefit of working with a partner that can help with execution of the contract while letting the small business earn critical proven performance and position them competitively for future work. Said differently, the small business gets the contract win, but subcontracts the bulk of the work to the more capable and efficient large company (Figure 8.1).

Large vs. Small Business

My research drew from participants whose companies fit all size categories: small, medium, and large. It's difficult to categorize precisely how many of which type of company lobby, as the numbers are available in

FIGURE 8.1
The Big Prime can also be a sub-contractor.

ways that require comparisons across disparate data sets, and the data are demonstrably incomplete. Existing research focuses on various aspects of the defense and lobbying ecosystem: small business, contracting, campaign finance, the revolving door, *etc.*

One can look into the Lobbying Disclosure Act (LDA) database to identify those companies registered to lobby. Using that data alone, Open Secrets identifies 1,765 companies registered to lobby defense issues in 2022. As identified in Chapter 2, these secondary data are only as good as the lobbying filings from which the number derives. As identified in Chapter 7, only some companies register as required.

When one looks at the annual national defense authorization act (NDAA), or defense appropriations bill, thousands of edits to the President's budget submission appear. Some changes are significant, adding or subtracting tens or hundreds of millions of dollars, and in some cases, billions of dollars. At the smaller end of the scale, the pencil dust and rounding errors in the eyes of some are the changes of single-digit millions, plus or minus.

Those changes reflect adjustments approved and conferenced by the House and Senate defense committees, a right inherent in Congress' power of the purse. It would take extraordinary research to reverse engineer the origins of every plus or minus made by Congress to these substantial pieces of legislation. However, we can deduce based on the budget lines and programs affected that many of those adjustments go to other than the very largest companies. They are too small for a large company to pursue yet substantial in the eyes of a smaller company.

How do I know this? Because it's a part of my role as a lobbyist to help companies advocate for this type of adjustment that will better position them for a contract award. I support companies of all sizes using the same techniques and communications messages regardless of the company's size. I know this because I have worked inside the process in industry, in Congress, and within the Department of Defense.

Large defense companies are followed and reported through national security press, defense media outlets, and public financial reporting. The top 200 winners of federal contracts across all of government (not just defense) are tracked annually by Bloomberg Government.[6] Number 200 on the list in 2019 had revenues approaching $7 billion. All companies in the Bloomberg Government 200 Federal Industry Leaders of 2019 are large businesses with revenues above one billion dollars; nearly all engage in lobbying.

Using quantitative analysis of a survey sampling of over 681 small businesses selling to DoD, Schilling et al. confirmed the presence of barriers to entry evident in the execution phase (acquisition and contracting).[7] Research and DoD's reporting to Congress on progress toward reaching small business goals confirm that over 80% of contract awards flow to other than small business.

The legislative adjustments referred to are primarily small in dollar value. Therefore, these budget adjustments don't significantly change the overall dynamic—relatively few large companies win most of the work and federal dollars. If companies of all sizes can interact with Congress to promote change, what difference does the type of business make when considering approaching Congress?

Type of Business

My research suggests that defense executives of *service* businesses need to see the federal sales opportunity to include congressional engagement like an executive of a product or manufacturing company. Differences in margins, commoditization of offerings, and competition force defense executives of service companies to look inward to identify areas for improvement vice outward. Defense executives of companies associated with products or manufacturing see engagement with Congress as an opportunity, where those associated with service companies do not.

One small business president in the software sector said,

> These big folks have lots of dollars, and if you look at their rate cards compared to others, they demand a premium. A lot of that premium is built on relationships. In the commercial world, obviously there's a lot of things that restrict government employees from spending a lot of time or accepting any gifts, but it is that time that's spent at that executive level with the senior folks, and I'm not just talking to SES [Senior Executive Service] folks, but it's those senior folks, they make sure they're walking. It's the same in the commercial world. Walking the hallways, being visible, having a conversation over coffee with somebody in the technical area and talk about capabilities in the marketplace or capabilities that could be brought to their agency.

His words reinforced the perception that personnel resources are required to spend the time cultivating the relationships and the future work.

Another research participant identified size with an ability to distribute resources toward contacts and relationships this way.

> So, I think the larger companies have a very large B.D. [business development] and capture staff. And so, they're able to put the resources, then, into pursuing many opportunities. I think that they spend a lot of time, probably, in D.C., then, talking with those various customers. Or if those customers are not in D.C., they spend a lot of time with them. Generally, they will hire people who have come from those particular commands.

The phrase "come from those commands" is a description of the revolving door with executives moving from an agency to industry (Chapter 1).

Executives carry preconceptions and perceptions of the relevance of company size and the impact of the engagement with a member of Congress. One president of a Virginia-based service business, commenting specifically on the calculus of engaging Congress said this:

> I don't think it would hurt as we are now as a company growing and now have a[n] office in Utah, for example, not a huge office, but a decent size office and starting to get offices in other places. I think it would help if we engage those elected representatives in those states. I don't think if we were to engage the Virginia congressional delegation or... D.C. really didn't have one... but Virginia, I mean, they wouldn't even come pay any attention to us. They're worried about Huntington [Ingalls] down in Norfolk and the great big guys, GDIT [General Dynamics Information Technologies] and those kind of companies, Lockheed Martin who has a 3,000-foot person footprint out in Manassas, [Virginia] stuff like that. I'm not sure it would help us at all in D.C. It might in Utah.

Some companies view the federal opportunity as a number game, pursuing multiple opportunities simultaneously, knowing that some percentage of those opportunities will yield a win. One research participant, a president of a service provider with multiple facilities observed the following fact:

> The companies that do things differently, I believe are using, many more lines in the water, if you will. They've got multiple, multiple business opportunities out there. Fairly large business development organizations that are pursuing 30, 40, 50 opportunities at any given time. And you win some and you lose some.

In my research, the concepts of size and type of business were relatively few compared to awareness, outcomes, and investment. However, all research participants referenced size and type as relevant to how they perceive their competitive landscape. They are factors to be considered, yet they don't prevent fuller participation. Their executives' perception that they can't participate prevents smaller and service businesses' participation. This assumes that they have sufficient awareness of the opportunity and process to begin with!

SUMMARY

In Chapter 8, I describe how the federal government categorizes businesses, funding, and support in the competitive environment. Further, I explore how evidence from bills that authorize and appropriate contract funds suggests that companies of all sizes can approach Congress to advocate changes. Yet the ultimate distribution of federal dollars favors large businesses. In Chapter 9, I'll describe how this condition reflects negatively on the very performance of democracy. We learn at an early age that democracy is fair. Let's peel this back.

NOTES

1 Ferris, S. P., Houston, R., & Javakhadz, D. (2019). It is a sweetheart of a Deal: Political connections and corporate-federal contracting. *Financial Review, 54*(1), 57–84, and Ridge, J. W., Ingram, A., & Hill, A. D. (2017). Beyond lobbying expenditures: How lobbying breadth and political connectedness affect firm outcomes. *Academy of Management Journal, 60*(3), 1138–1163.

2 See PL 117–328, https://www.govinfo.gov/content/pkg/COMPS-1834/pdf/COMPS-1834.pdf.

3 See https://www.sba.gov/federal-contracting/contracting-guide/types-contracts.

4 Krusemark, T., & Wayne, W. (2019) Service-disabled veteran-owned small business perceptions of subcontracting training within the department of defense. *Walden Dissertations and Doctoral Studies*, 7548. https://scholarworks.waldenu.edu/dissertations/7548.

5 The actual size of the industrial base is not indeed known. Various sources identify a number between 100,000 companies and over one million companies. There are countless companies registered as legal entities but that do not compete for

federal work. Further, many companies enter, fail, and rotate out of the market without fanfare. Academic research consistently recognizes 350,000 is a generally accepted number of companies actively participating in the defense industrial base. Industry trade groups annually report numbers that often do not align with academic research findings.

6 Bloomberg Government. (2020). BGOV 200. *Federal industry leaders 2019.*
7 Schilling, R. (2017). *Analysis of perceived challenges experienced by small businesses competing for department of defense contracts.* www.proquest.com%2Fdissertations-theses%2Fanalysis-perceived-challenges-experienced-small%2Fdocview%2F18713 15971%2Fse-2%3Faccountid%3D1487.

9

The Polarities of Democracy: Applying a Theoretical Lens

This chapter is different from the rest of the book as it brings the reader to a theoretical perspective on the business of government goods and services. The focus shifts to a much higher plane to observe the competitive landscape in the context of the performance of our democratic institutions. It would be easy to skip this chapter; *I encourage you to resist that temptation.* Challenge yourself to view your own business dynamic and relationship to supporting the government buyer in a manner unique to our nation's ongoing experiment with democracy. This chapter draws on my original research in the interest of challenging the reader to step outside of the competitive business environment to examine systemic issues inherent in government sales.

In the United States our public discourse surrounding politics is in a particularly stressed state. Ideology, social issues, and incoherent yet continuous information flows conspire to make it easier for some to look away and ignore government activities in Washington, DC. In federal sales, we look away from the process to our detriment. This chapter will lift the reader's sights from the din of hyperactive cable news channels, subscription inbox news alerts, push notifications, and unhelpful opinions of friend circles. Providers of goods and services to the federal government should reasonably expect fair processes for the buying and selling of those goods and services.

Given the information to this point in the book, along with your own understanding of the competitive landscape, one might question whether the institutions that implement the federal sales process are really conforming to our democratic ideals? Does the federal funding and acquisition

DOI: 10.4324/9781003454885-9

process that leads to your sales execute fairly such that any company qualified to produce a good, service or solution can compete on a level playing field? To what degree may we be accepting an imbalance of winners and losers as "just the way it is?"

FRAMEWORKS

My qualitative research is grounded in both a conceptual and theoretical framework. I'll describe how the two frameworks fit together before describing how they inform my research findings that were the themes of prior chapters. Barry Johnson's conceptual framework of polarity management[1] focuses on the recognition and management of unsolvable problems.

Conceptual Theory

Johnson describes that a polarity exists if a problem is unsolvable and has two interdependent poles, positive and negative. A solvable problem may be resolved through either/or thinking. However, an unsolvable problem is actually a polarity with two interrelated poles, each dependent on the other to some degree. Because they are polarities, they will go on in perpetuity and must be managed. Such polarities are, by definition, unsolvable. A polarity contains two *interdependent* poles and each has both positive and negative aspects in varying states of tension. When recognizing the problem's chronic nature, managing the poles allows one to leverage the positive attributes of both poles of a polarity to achieve the best outcomes while minimizing the effects of the polarity's negative attributes.

THE ONGOING NATURE OF THE PROBLEM

The interdependent nature of the two poles allows for the perpetual movement between the positive and negative attributes of each pole. Polarity Partnerships, LLC has developed a very useful polarity map as seen in Figure 9.1. For illustrative purposes only, the figure identifies two poles, each with positive and negative aspects as shown in the upper (positive)

Action Steps
How will we gain or maintain
the positive results from focusing
on this left pole? What? Who?
By When? Measures?

Action Steps
How will we gain or maintain
the positive results from focusing
on this right pole? What? Who?
By When? Measures?

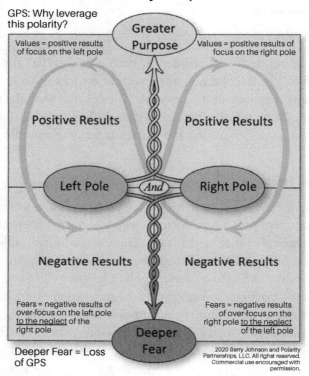

Polarity Map®

Image reproduced with permission of Polarity Partnerships, LLC and the Institute for the Polarities of Democracy.

Early Warnings
Measurable indicators (things you
can count) that will let you know
that you are getting into the
downside of this left pole.

Early Warnings
Measurable indicators (things you
can count) that will let you know
that you are getting into the
downside of this right pole.

FIGURE 9.1
Polarity map template.

and lower (negative) quadrants. The positives of each pole appear in the upper quadrants, and the negatives appear in the lower quadrants. The upper and lower bubbles, in this case, refer to the very best or very worst outcome of a polarity.

The infinity loop reflects that the polarity goes on forever. Managing the polarity in a manner that promotes the positives and reduces the negatives suggests that the infinity loop best sits well above the horizontal axis. The areas outside the four quadrants indicate either action steps that could promote positives, or early warning signs that are indicators of the negatives of the respective pole. This template is adaptable to any polarity. Before proceeding to the framework's use in my research findings, I'll demonstrate the map using a polarity we all live with: breathing!

A Polarity in Everyday Living

Figure 9.2 demonstrates the polarity of breathing. To sustain life, one must manage breathing by both inhaling and exhaling. Breathing doesn't happen with only one action, and it's a condition that must be managed. It is an *either/or* solution of life and death. However, to sustain life, the polarity of inhaling *and* exhaling must work interdependently to manage the positive values of the polarity. Fortunately for humans, management of this condition takes place automatically such that we don't have to think about it. The highest purpose of breathing is to sustain life (the top of the map). The deepest fear is death (the bottom of the map). Within the upper quadrants are the positives of the polarity.

In normal daily living, we don't think about breathing. However, if we decide to run a marathon, we'll need to work more consciously to manage this polarity. Building up lung capacity and the supporting cardio-pulmonary strength will help assure that the polarity's positives are more pronounced than the negatives. Building a balance of endurance and speed are action steps that move us toward the polarity's positives. Issues such as cramping or fatigue might appear as early warning signs indicating movement toward the polarity's negatives.

Theoretical Framework

The theoretical framework for the research is William Benet's Polarities of Democracy.[2] The Polarities of Democracy is a useful framework for

Action Steps
How will we gain or maintain the positive results from focusing on this left pole? What? Who? By When? Measures?

Action Steps
How will we gain or maintain the positive results from focusing on this right pole? What? Who? By When? Measures?

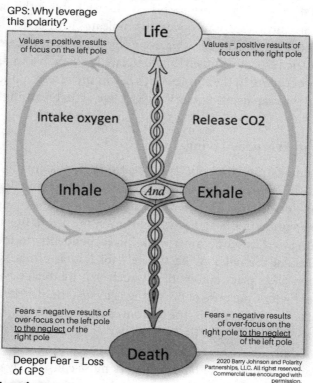

Polarity Map®

GPS: Why leverage this polarity?

Values = positive results of focus on the left pole

Values = positive results of focus on the right pole

Life

Intake oxygen

Release CO_2

Inhale *And* Exhale

Fears = negative results of over-focus on the left pole to the neglect of the right pole

Fears = negative results of over-focus on the right pole to the neglect of the left pole

Deeper Fear = Loss of GPS

Death

Early Warnings
Measurable indicators (things you can count) that will let you know that you are getting into the downside of this left pole.

Early Warnings
Measurable indicators (things you can count) that will let you know that you are getting into the downside of this right pole.

FIGURE 9.2
Polarity map—breathing.

examining democracy's promise and confirms there can be multiple explanations for the underperformance of a democracy. Benet demonstrates that democracy is an either/or solution to the problem of oppression and achieving self-governance. To effectively achieve the either/or solution of democracy requires the use of both/and thinking that polarity management provides.

When the conceptual and theoretical frameworks are used together, polarity management allows the effective leveraging of five polarity pairs of the Polarities of Democracy. Benet identifies 10 values that form five polarity pairs that are present and must be addressed if democracy is to fulfill its promise. According to Benet, no pair works alone, and each of the five pairs has some interdependence with the other pairs. The five polarity pairs within the Polarities of Democracy are:

> freedom and authority
> justice and due process
> diversity and equality
> human rights and communal obligations
> participation and representation

Applying this theoretical lens allows one to see competitive inequities the lobbying condition amplifies, such as fewer than 1% of companies registered to lobby at the federal level, and relatively few winners outmaneuvering the competition *via* legislative funding and policy decisions. In my research this theory proves useful in focusing on polarities specifically relevant to the federal sales, participation and representation, and diversity and equality.

Benet understands democracy as a solution to oppression.[3] Oppression can take multiple forms, and Benet's theoretical model proves inherently flexible in examining oppression across government institutions as diverse as immigration policy,[4] homogeneity of social capital,[5] and care of military adolescent children.[6] Similar to one of Benet's stated beliefs of oppression, my research focuses on whether "structural oppression",[7] is evident in the perceptions of defense executives. For the purpose of my research and this book, I consider the control aspect of oppression rather than the more common social justice understanding of oppression. Oppression can take multiple forms in society, the workplace, and government performance for its citizens. Benet identifies the existence of oppression and the desire to limit its influence as a force that drives the pursuit of democracy. By extension, the performance of government institutions directly influences the speed at which democratization can take place. Democracy remains an unfinished pursuit, and the "positive and negative attributes"[8] of its polarity values can be managed to get the best of the interdependent poles.

In recognizing the inherent tensions of the interactions of the opposing poles, Benet's adaptation of Johnson's concept is a valuable tool in examining the ongoing challenges of implementing democracy's promise. Such is the case with businesses fully participating in opportunities to shape and seek funding in the federal marketplace. Specifically, Benet's pairs of diversity and equality, and participation and representation, are evident throughout the lobbying dynamic identified in my research.

Applications of Theory

Benet's theoretical framework allows scholars to examine corporate lobbying on a higher plane and in the context of the very performance of democracy, above the influence peddling,[9] political giving,[10] campaign finance,[11] dark money,[12] and acquisition reform.[13] In federal sales, we see those who favor change (a challenge to technology or current practice), and those with interests in maintaining the status quo (incumbents). Consistent with Johnson, the actors of government (officeholders and agency or government decision-makers), and corporate defense executives associated with lobbying, can assume those roles to varying degrees. Firm-level lobbyists,[14] association and coalition advocates,[15] and revolving door lobbyists[16] all assume either role (favoring change or maintaining status quo) depending on the policy or programmatic condition under legislative consideration. Retaining power, influence, or competitive advantage motivates negative aspects of polarities in the context of democracy as incumbents preserve their position.

DIVERSITY AND EQUALITY

The diversity and equality polarity pair is helpful when exploring equality among government constituencies. In the case of defense executives, the constituencies include the individual, the corporation, and agencies of government. Using the polarity map, Figure 9.3 depicts diversity and

Action Steps
How will we gain or maintain
the positive results from focusing
on this left pole? What? Who?
By When? Measures?

Action Steps
How will we gain or maintain
the positive results from focusing
on this right pole? What? Who?
By When? Measures?

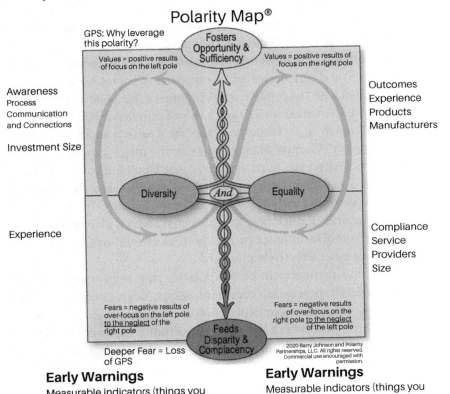

Polarity Map®

GPS: Why leverage
this polarity?

Fosters
Opportunity &
Sufficiency

Values = positive results
of focus on the left pole

Values = positive results of
focus on the right pole

Awareness
Process
Communication
and Connections

Investment Size

Outcomes
Experience
Products
Manufacturers

Diversity   *And*   Equality

Experience

Compliance
Service
Providers
Size

Fears = negative results of
over-focus on the left pole
to the neglect of the
right pole

Fears = negative results
of over-focus on the
right pole to the neglect
of the left pole

Feeds
Disparity &
Complacency

Deeper Fear = Loss
of GPS

2020 Barry Johnson and Polarity
Partnerships, LLC. All right reserved.
Commercial use encouraged with
permission.

Early Warnings
Measurable indicators (things you
can count) that will let you know
that you are getting into the
downside of this left pole.

Early Warnings
Measurable indicators (things you
can count) that will let you know
that you are getting into the
downside of this right pole.

FIGURE 9.3
Polarity map of diversity and equality polarity pair.

equality forming the left and right poles respectively. The upper bubble indicates the greater purpose statement of the polarity to "foster opportunity and sufficiency".[17] The lower bubble indicates the deepest fears of the polarity to "feed disparity and complacency".[18]

The presence of high awareness, effective communications, and established connections (all described in Chapter 3) all support actions associated with attaining the positive aspects of diversity through which unique solutions to government needs can be brought forward. Defense executives of companies of sufficient size (Chapter 8), and capable of making investments (Chapter 5), are best able to pursue opportunities associated with this polarity's highest purpose. Similarly, defense executives of manufacturers or product companies (Chapter 8), who also possess the requisite experience (Chapter 6) and can foresee future outcomes (Chapter 4), can promote action associated with the positive opportunities of this polarity pair.

Conversely, a defense executive's low levels of experience (Chapter 6) and awareness (Chapter 3), or executives associated with a small or service-oriented company (Chapter 8), suggest early warning signs of the negatives of this polarity pair. Such early warning signs indicate conditions of movement away from the positives above, and toward the negatives more closely associated with disparities and complacency. The themes are not directly inverse. Rather they are subjective, which also makes them suitable for possible techniques such as policies or methods by which the polarity can be more effectively managed.

In the effective management of this polarity pair, improving a defense executive's level of awareness, communications, degrees of connection, perspective on outcomes, and experience, the conditions exist for movement toward the positives of the pair (opportunity and sufficiency) and away from the negatives. Failure to improve the areas reflected by each of these themes will increase the likelihood of movement toward the negatives (disparities and complacency).

PARTICIPATION AND REPRESENTATION

Defense executives, like all citizens, can choose the degree to which they participate in the legislative processes of democracy. Benet describes this polarity pair as one of both "function and meaning".[19] The act of lobbying relates to function, and the regenerative quality of choosing when to participate invokes the meaning of the polarity. Citizens have a right to choose to what degree they might participate in government. Some issues are of more significance to citizens and may garner more interest than others. The naming of a post office versus changes to social security eligibility for example.

Figure 9.4 adapts the polarity map template that serves this polarity pair as it serves all polarity pairs, with upper quadrants reflecting positives and lower quadrants reflecting negatives. Participation and representation both form the left and right pole, respectively. The upper bubble indicates the highest purpose of this pair, maximizing the positive aspects of "productive

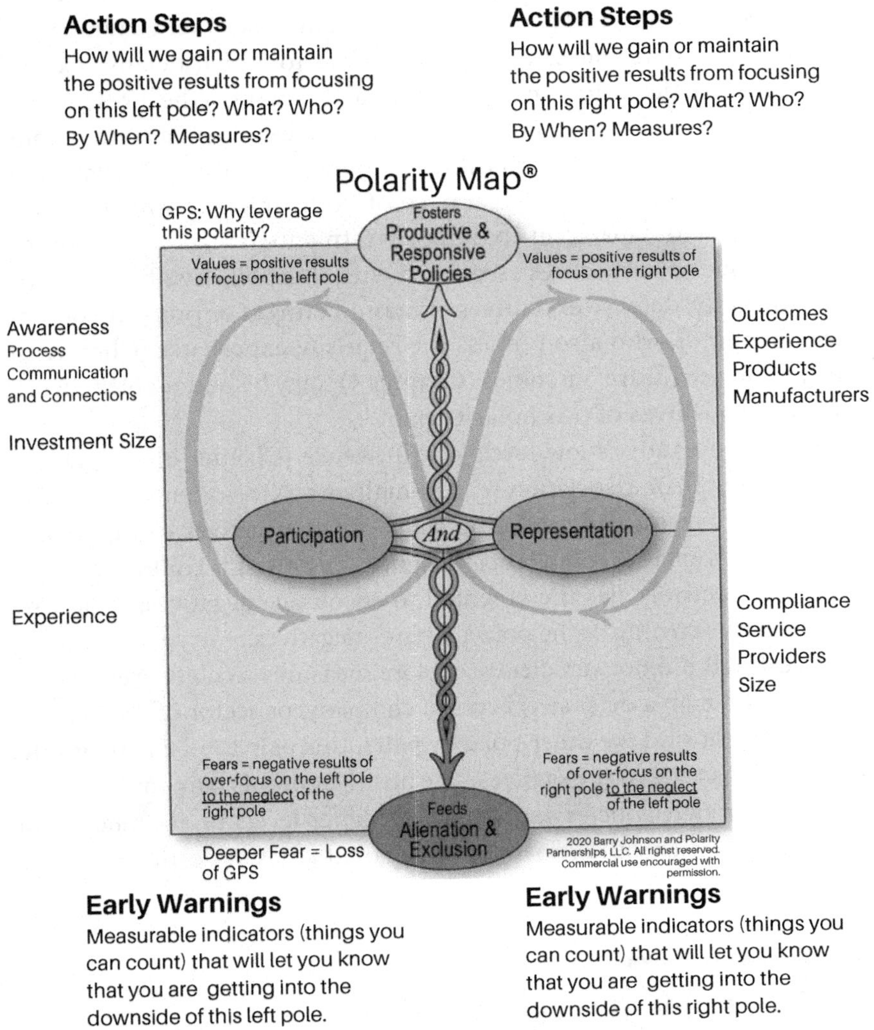

Action Steps

How will we gain or maintain the positive results from focusing on this left pole? What? Who? By When? Measures?

Action Steps

How will we gain or maintain the positive results from focusing on this right pole? What? Who? By When? Measures?

Polarity Map®

GPS: Why leverage this polarity?

Fosters Productive & Responsive Policies

Values = positive results of focus on the left pole

Values = positive results of focus on the right pole

Awareness
Process
Communication
and Connections

Investment Size

Outcomes
Experience
Products
Manufacturers

Participation *And* Representation

Experience

Compliance
Service
Providers
Size

Fears = negative results of over-focus on the left pole to the neglect of the right pole

Fears = negative results of over-focus on the right pole to the neglect of the left pole

Feeds Alienation & Exclusion

Deeper Fear = Loss of GPS

2020 Barry Johnson and Polarity Partnerships, LLC. All rights reserved. Commercial use encouraged with permission.

Early Warnings

Measurable indicators (things you can count) that will let you know that you are getting into the downside of this left pole.

Early Warnings

Measurable indicators (things you can count) that will let you know that you are getting into the downside of this right pole.

Image reproduced with permission of Polarity Partnerships, LLC and the Institute for the Polarities of Democracy.

FIGURE 9.4

Polarity map of participation and representation polarity pair.

and responsive policies"[20] while minimizing the negative aspects. The lower bubble indicates the deepest fears of the polarity pair, "alienation or exclusion"[21] where the negatives are maximized and the positives are minimized. The infinity loop in each of Figures 9.1–9.4 represents the perpetual nature of the ongoing need for management of the polarity. In the case of the figures shown, the infinity loop represents a well-managed polarity staying high in the positive quadrants and hardly dipping at all into the lower quadrants.

My research data indicate varying degrees to which defense executives value participation in congressional lobbying. The presence of high awareness, effective communications, and established connections (all in Chapter 3) allow for conditions supportive of this polarity pair's positives. Further, defense executives of companies of sufficient size (Chapter 8), and capable of making investments (Chapter 5), may be able to pursue opportunities associated with this polarity's highest purpose. Similarly, defense executives of manufacturers or product companies (Chapter 8), who also possess the requisite experience (Chapter 6) and can foresee future outcomes (Chapter 4), may be better able to work toward the positives of this polarity pair.

A defense executive's low levels of experience (Chapter 6) and awareness (Chapter 3), or association with a small or service-oriented company (Chapter 8), suggest early warning signs of the negatives of this polarity pair. Additionally, compliance (Chapter 7), through conformance or absence respectively, has the potential to encourage negatives, or at least indicate early warning of the polarity pair's negatives.

The research did not sufficiently explore measures to objectively report where on the map a defense executive, company, or sector of the defense industry might sit. Like other polarity pairs, this pair can be managed to encourage positives over negatives. The positives of this pair could be best managed through policies supportive of higher levels of awareness and access, as well as encouragement of transparent communications.

MOVING FORWARD FROM THEORY

Unsolvable problems, or problems with multiple possible solutions, can be most effectively managed when the polarity is managed to maximize the positives and minimize the negatives.[22] When defense executives exercise the decision to lobby Congress, managing these positives supports the furtherance of the promise of democracy through equitable legislation and subsequent fair competition.

As described in Chapters 1 and 2, it is the positioning of funding and statements of policy in legislation that ultimately support the award of government contracts. The democratization of the interconnected processes that lead to a contract appears to fall short without further participation in congressional lobbying. When defense executives fail to exercise the decision to lobby Congress, conditions exist that allow the negatives of the polarity pairs to affect government's performance.

SO WHAT?

In Chapters 1 and 2, I describe the complex environment in which the decision to lobby Congress takes place. The orchestrated sequence of the budget cycle requires that defense executives synthesize business, government, and political implications in considering the likelihood of specific outcomes lobbying might support. The interpretation of this complex environment goes beyond the basics of following the budget document for a given fiscal year from the executive to the legislature and back to the executive. The findings of the research confirm that understanding whether, where, or when to insert oneself into the process requires various levels of awareness, experience, and ability to foresee potential outcomes and returns on investments, all within a system of rules governing such decisions and communications.

It is the positioning of funding and statements of policy in legislation that ultimately support the award of government contracts. The democratization of the interconnected processes that lead to a contract appears to fall short without further participation in congressional lobbying. When defense executives fail to exercise the decision to lobby Congress, conditions exist that allow the negatives of the polarity pairs to affect government's performance.

The themes and subthemes emerging from the data represent perceived facilitators of and barriers to the defense executives' decision to lobby Congress. The use of semi-structured interviews allowed the data to emerge without asking the research question directly of the participants. In doing so, the questions elicited responses that revealed the executives' level of understanding of this complex environment, allowing me to examine their words and subsequently interpret their perceptions. The polarity maps help the reader visualize the theoretical implications of defense executives' understanding of the complex environment in which the federal sale eventually takes place.

IMPLICATIONS FOR PRACTICE

Multiple academic studies confirm a decades-long effort by Congress to address defense acquisition reform. There is no evidence that confirms such emphasis has been applied to the understanding and use of the relationship between business and Congress as has been applied to the relationship of business and the executive branch. My research findings support the need to better identify and set conditions to improve executive levels of knowledge. Such improvements would allow understanding of the role of Congress in federal funding, policy, and contracts, and perhaps support the effective management of the polarity pairs considered. Congress should consider incorporating these findings into practical policies that might encourage defense executives' improved levels of awareness. Congress is well positioned to set conditions that allow for more effective management of polarity pairs that will allow greater democratization and move closer to fulfillment of the promise of democracy.

My research represents a first probe in attempting to understand facilitators of or barriers to defense executives' decision to lobby Congress, and was specific to companies with revenues between $5 million and $1 billion. The breadth of this criteria includes hundreds of thousands of defense companies. Themes described in earlier chapters, and framed above in theory, suggest there is room to improve executive levels of integrated process knowledge critical to positioning for best competitive outcomes during the budget execution phase.

The inter-relationships of awareness, process, communications and connection, investment, outcomes, and experience were evident throughout the data. Closer examination of specific aspects of each theme would further extend the research literature and further inform policy makers. Executive education and training could help elevate levels of knowledge of defense practitioners, and allow for fuller participation across the entire budget development process.

Budgeting, legislation, and federal contracting are each interrelated and practical aspects of the performance of democracy. My research attempts to look beyond large vs. small company comparisons, and was distinct from ongoing research and efforts in acquisition, campaign finance, and lobbying reforms. Understanding how defense executives perceive the environment in which they make the decision to lobby can inform all such reforms.

SUMMARY

Chapter 9 purposely focuses on the application of theory as a means of allowing the reader to see lobbying in the context of the performance of democracy and some of the relevant democratic institutions. The theoretical framework allows the reader to consider where lobbying fits into the democratic process without the baggage and negative affiliation often ascribed to the political acts of a relative few. When the themes of Chapters 2 through 8 are examined in the context of the theories in Chapter 9, the reader begins to see lobbying as a more natural part of the performance of democracy, and one we should take care to assure equal access to all. In Chapter 10, I'll present specific case studies of companies of all sizes and types whose leadership understood a process, recognized a future outcome, invested time and resources to influence, and achieved outcomes that would not have happened without thoughtful lobbying.

NOTES

1   Johnson, B. (1992). *Polarity management*. HRD Press.
2   Benet, W. J. (2013). Managing the polarities of democracy: A theoretical framework for positive social change. *Journal of Social Change, 5*(1), 26–39.
3   Hayes, N. (2019). *The effects of a multicultural overseas community on military adolescents*. www.proquest.com%2Fdissertations-theses%2Feffects-multicultural-overseas-community-on%2Fdocview%2F2228137493%2Fse-2%3Faccountid%3D14872.
4   Mcdaniel, R. (2019). *Metropolitan young adult american muslims perceptions of discrimination post American patriot act*. www.proquest.com%2Fdissertations-theses%2Fmetropolitan-young-adult-american-muslims%2Fdocview%2F2204934257%2Fse-2%3Faccountid%3D14872.
5   Strouble, B. (2015). *Racism vs. social capital: A case study of two majority black communities*. Walden University Scholar Works.
6   See footnote iii.

7 See footnote ii.

8 See footnote ii.

9 Hartung, W. D. (2019). Defense contractors are tightening their grip on our government. *The Nation*. https://www.thenation.com/article/archive/military-industrial-complex-defense-contractors-raytheon-united-technologies-merger/.

10 Scott, W. D. (2015). Investigating the need for transparent disclosures of political campaign contributions and lobbying ependitures by U.S. private prison corporations. *Accounting and the Public Interest*, *15*(1), 27–52. https://doi.org/10.2308/apin-51401.

11 Leys, N. (2021). "Masters of war"? The defense industry, the appearance of corruption, and the future of campaign finance. *Yale Law & Policy Review*.

12 Ibid.

13 Quinones, E., Jr. (2018). *U.S. government acquisition reform and its influence on defense contracting, innovation, diversification, and collaboration*. www.proquest.com%2Fdissertations-theses%2Fu-s-government-acquisition-reform-influence-on%2Fdocview%2F2201395012%2Fse-2%3Faccountid%3D14872 and Schwartz, M., & Peters, H. M. (2018). *Acquisition reform in the FY2016-FY2018 national defense authorization acts*. 1–23. https://dair.nps.edu/handle/123456789/4141.

14 Kim, I. S. (2017). Political cleavages within industry: Firm-level lobbying for trade liberalization. *American Political Science Review*, *111*(1), 1.

15 Hojnacki, M., Marchetti, K. M., Baumgartner, F. R., Berry, J. M., Kimball, D. C., & Leech, B. L. (2015). Assessing business advantage in Washington lobbying. *Interest Groups and Advocacy*, *4*(3), 2047–7414. https://doi.org/10.1057/iga.2015.3.

16 Chausow, L. E. (2015). *It's more than who you know: The role of access, procedural and policy expertise, and policy knowledge in revolving door lobbying* (Order No. 3663469). www.proquest.com%2Fdissertations-theses%2Fmore-than-who-you-know-role-access-procedural%2Fdocview%2F1701140194%2Fse-2%3Faccountid%3D14872 and Strickland, J. M. (2020). The declining value of revolving-door lobbyists: Evidence from the American States. *American Journal of Political Science*, *64*(1), 67–81. https://doi.org/10.1111/ajps.12485.

17 Benet, W. J., Keyser, W. C., & Rackl, S. E. (2022). *A set of basic maps for the polarities of democracy theory*. Institute for the Polarities of Democracy.

18 Ibid.

19 See footnote ii.

20 See footnote xvii.

21 See footnote xvii.

22 See footnote i.

10

Integrating Lobbying into Your Plan

Throughout the book, I identify explanations of budgeting, lobbying, executive understanding, compliance, and ever-present systemic challenges surrounding the environment of federal sales. I also demonstrate a perspective of lobbying and its impact on the performance of democracy, inferring that we may needlessly accept the status quo as "just the way it is" and contribute to democracy's underperformance with an acquisition system geared to reward the most sophisticated participants.

Integrating a technical understanding of the process, timing, and messaging required across the budget development and execution spectrum, those able to synthesize process knowledge with ever-present and changing environmental dynamics achieve preferred outcomes. Using the defense industry as a primary example where the winners truly master the overarching process, I suggest that other industries could also attain heightened access and better outcomes if they could increase their awareness, imagine better outcomes, and make those outcomes a reality.

The complexity of the federal sales environment is a barrier of its own. In the interest of protecting taxpayer dollars, our government collectively establishes costly and convoluted law and policy that achieves the inverse outcome—we spend enormous energy on extraordinary processes that continually build on the preceding interpretations of law and policy. Decades of acquisition reform serve to only further confuse new entrants. Better Buying Power 1.0, 2.0, and 3.0, for example, put words and plans to an elusive goal of improving acquisition efficiency. Yet the reforms have not made a dramatic improvement on outputs or the access by new and innovative companies many such improvements require.

The Small Business Administration, a well-intended, reasonably well-funded, and sprawling agency, exists in some form throughout the executive branch. Left unaddressed by the SBA is the critical legislative phase, overseen by the co-equal government branch, our Congress. The time the budget spends in Congress, notionally from the first Monday in February through the start of the new fiscal year October 1, amounts to nearly one-third of the budget's time in development. In the past decade, the budget has only been completed on time once, thereby increasing the time spent on the Hill. Most budgets go well into the new fiscal year they must fund before final passage. There is no equivalent of the SBA to help companies understand how to navigate Congress during this dynamic phase of the budgets' critique, markup, and final passage.

The top-performing federal contractors consistently engage Congress with appropriately registered lobbyists, a deliberate plan, and a meaningful message. This happens partly because we effectively cede meaningful access enshrined in our constitution, the First Amendment's "right of redress," to only those who understand the opaque and needlessly obscure process effective congressional communications requires. Is this intentional on the part of Congress? It would appear so, but I contend that this condition exists, in part, because it has gone without serious examination.

Previous academic research of lobbying focuses on perspectives and data from lobbyists or Congress people, campaign finance, and lobbying reporting. Each source comes with constraints that limit complete understanding. When examining the perspectives of those who decide to lobby the most considerable portion of the discretionary federal budget, defense, my research identifies shortcomings in executives' abilities to synthesize the necessary information.

Most Senators and Congress people would proclaim that their doors are always open to constituents and public groups. That is indeed nearly universally true. Constituent services, responding to requests for support with benefits, for example, consume numerous hours and produce thousands of pages of correspondence annually. However, a company needing to gain knowledge of how to seek support or explain the value of products and services in a meaningful way, to the correct decision-makers, at the right time and place in Congress will routinely lose to companies that possess such knowledge.

Throughout *Government Deals Are Funded, Not Sold*, we've seen how the linkages of awareness, process knowledge, communications, networks, connections, investment, and imagining of better outcomes one must precisely orchestrate to have an impact. Today, as has been the case for over two centuries, one must know someone, have prior experience, or know how to hire a specialized guide, a lobbyist.

Given the systematic review of the lobbying dynamic by Congress, an opportunity exists to apply new thinking to promoting the executive awareness necessary to increase meaningful access. Policies, courses, seminars, and open houses, funded and promoted by Congress, could help. Congress could and should better explain how to participate in the legislative process to the masses.

Liaison offices exist in every agency to promote communication between Congress and the Executive branch. SBA offices exist across the executive branch to promote communication and entry to the executive branch. No such common entry point exists within Congress for more direct industry access. My research confirms those inside the Beltway bubble may take their accumulated on-the-job training as common knowledge across the industry. If this condition exists in the defense industry, it also exists in other industries.

Throughout the book, I've tied concepts together to encourage executives of any industry to feel more confident in approaching the critical legislative phase of federal sales. In the following pages are case studies of companies of all sizes with whom I have provided advice, counsel, and guidance, helping them achieve essential changes in policy and funding that at once served the federal customer need while enhancing bottom lines. Finally, I will close the book with a smattering of observations that could help any executive improve by learning from others. *I wish you only success as you Get Funded!*

11

Case Studies

A wooden labyrinth maze game was once popular with children. By tilting the maze in two dimensions, the object is to move a steel ball through an identifiable path to the finish. Companies of all sizes can recognize the game's parallels with pursuing a government contract. Lobbying can tilt the opportunity maze depending on one's perspective. Executives of companies that don't lobby may feel the effects of the tilted maze but need to recognize why the opportunity is tilted to favor some over others. Conversely, executives of companies that do lobby are carefully orchestrating movements that will generate subsequent outcomes through contracts and favorable policies—tilted in their favor. This chapter offers examples of how companies of all sizes can influence outcomes, large and small. Are you maneuvering the metal ball through the labyrinth, or are you just hanging on hoping to prevent motion sickness while getting to the end of the maze? (Figure 11.1)

FIGURE 11.1
The labyrinth game.

DOI: 10.4324/9781003454885-11

Case Study—US Air Force

SITUATION

A mid-sized technology company was successfully garnering the attention of the US Air Force and landing repeated SBIR contracts. Their prior success selling to state government was translating to federal sales. Although the wins were beginning to stack up across multiple programs, the individual contract values were relatively small. It's common to see SBIR contracts awarded in low millions or hundreds of thousands of dollars. The company knew they needed to generate more attention for their technology if they were to convince the US Air Force to invest more thoroughly and help the US Air Force to improve its condition to the degree their commercial counterparts have advanced with the same technologies.

INTERVENTION

Together, we mapped the funding that supports the multiple SBIR contracts. Pulling these threads revealed the real US Air Force customer. The company thought one office controlled the purse strings; however, a more focused research process revealed multiple agency decision-makers in the funding process. With the emergence of the US Space Force, ownership of several programs was complex for those in industry to identify. This is primarily because budget lines between the two services had yet to settle in the newly established US Space Force organization finally. Not surprisingly, sometimes, US Air Force and US Space Force would conflict with ownership of a funding line.

The company and I developed a more comprehensive story of US Air Force's needs. We shared a proposal to consolidate funding in one place for this capability and this company's offering. With US Air Force support for a more streamlined approach, we took the proposal to congressional decision-makers seeking their support to adjust funding appropriately.

OUTCOME

By sharing information with relevant stakeholders in the funding decisions, we strengthened support for a specific technical capability more appropriately resourced to help the warfighters. Congress positioned more funding to support capabilities requiring this company's technology. It is common for funding lines to shift, particularly during an agency reorganization. Rather than waiting for the dust to settle on a reorganization, they brought the better funding methodology forward.

Applying specific process knowledge to a critical technology use case allowed this company to better position itself within the subsequent acquisition and contract processes. They shaped the best outcome for the company and the US Air Force customer and convinced the US Air Force to invest more fully in their technology.

Case Study—National Security Policy with China

HOW ONE SMALL COMPANY CHANGED FEDERAL POLICY

This true story stems from one company's desire to help the United States achieve a better solution and help the national security posture with a specific challenge, even though this company was a tiny fish in a vast and busy pond.

This single company was able to influence a policy issue that had both national and international security importance. This story shows that despite the complexity of the process, anyone has access to the federal government and can influence a policy change. The complexity can be better understood when seen as appropriate and more simplified tasks. And the tasks take place across the 3-Ring Circus of Federal Sales[SM]: Industry, Agency, and Congress. This one company participated in all three rings at the highest level and made a difference.

THE PROBLEMS WELL-MEANING POLICY CAN CAUSE

The company of this story is a magnet manufacturer. They make highly specialized magnets using materials that come from rare earth materials. Rare earth elements often have unusual names like dysprosium, samarium, and neodymium.

The magnets this company makes use neodymium, which comes from only a few places in the world. There was a time when you could get it in the United States, but now it almost all comes from China; a minimal amount comes from Australia. Neodymium gets processed in other countries before it fits into final articles. It applies to very specialized needs in the defense industry.

The US Congress wanted to avoid relying on a Chinese-derived supply chain for particular defense articles. Consequently, Congress determined that the United States would no longer allow defense suppliers to source from supply chains that used material originating from China. Although that law achieved a specific desired end state, it didn't allow for a transition period for suppliers to reconfigure their supply chains. It made political sense but needed to make more practical sense. In short, the policy hampered the United States in the short term while envisioning an ideological break from reliance on China.

The situation—A well-intended end-state to reduce reliance on critical supplies from a foreign nation and potential adversary did not allow for a transition period from the current practices, which overlooked the conflicting requirement of qualified supply chains. This is a remarkably complex problem in defense because a supply chain must first qualify through the US Government, which can take a long time—sometimes years.

Unlike an average American buyer who can switch buying their detergent from Walmart to Target, in the defense world, a supplier can't just change from buying from Joe to buying from Bill; the process is more complex and lengthier. Although Congress thought they were taking a firm stand in writing that law, it forced a policy that was not executable. And if you're the supplier in the supply chain and you provide a product, you may be the only one who understands the new law's real impact.

ACHIEVING POSITIVE OUTCOMES DESPITE THE ODDS—ENTER OUR HERO

The magnet manufacturer in our story is four layers down from the prime vendor of a significant platform. This company recognized the problem immediately: If we can't deliver the highly specialized magnets on the time sequence that they're needed, this will be a problem for delivering the magnets to the major platform on time. Schedule delays impose extraordinary costs and, occasionally, national security risks.

This company recognized that only a few people would understand the technical issues and their consequences. Therefore, the company stepped back and evaluated their situation. They understood where they were in the industry ring. There are only a couple of companies who even participate in this market. They understood where they were in the pecking order of a prime and subprime contractor relationship. And those in defense understand that subprimes usually have different kinds of authority to directly communicate with the government customer.

So, the company attempted to communicate the problem through the supply chain. Unfortunately, they needed help to get the gravity of the issue to be correctly understood by the senior levels in the prime supply chain. The company president thought this was a potential national security concern and was willing to take a little risk.

The decision—With a substantial revenue stream at risk and an apparent national security dilemma before them, the company president made what he saw as the obvious choice to rock the boat.

Consequently, the company and I discussed who and where the potential agency communications points might be. In this case, we considered the agency customer, the Navy, but recognized that the prime vendors typically prefer to avoid subcontractors communicating with the Navy customer. The company recognized that, because this was an industrial base issue, the Office of the Secretary of Defense's Office of Industrial Base Policy should have a more significant concern here than just the one program at stake because potentially multiple programs would be affected by this. Therefore, we sought an audience with the Assistant Secretary of Defense for Industrial Base Policy. We were successful in describing the situation and what could take place.

Over time, we were able to convince the Office of Industrial Base Policy to work with us in communicating the severity of this issue, both to Congress and to others in the executive branch, in this case, Navy program officials and Navy acquisition officials. In addition, because it was a high-visibility national security concern that conflicted with publicly stated China policies, there was a reason for the White House Office of Trade Policy to be involved. White House officials were involved in China policy on a much broader scale, making sweeping generalizations about how China policy would unfold. Consequently, this issue needed to be flagged as one that might warrant an exception to this well-intended policy.

We successfully communicated with the White House Office of Trade Policy and received multiple audiences to discuss alternatives and possible solutions. The result of those conversations between the White House and the Office of the Secretary of Defense was the transmission of a Presidential Decision Directive (PDD). A highly unusual memo from the President to the supply chain and the Office of the Secretary of Defense stated a unique need for this type of material required to make magnets. That allowed maneuvering room and space for policymakers to find a workaround for this policy so that we could eventually get to the intent of what Congress had meant for the law and ease away from reliance on a product originating from China, which would take several years.

Get Funded—Policy solutions often create second-order effects. You and your company may be the first to recognize a policy problem.

Policy can be a law, agency policy, or sometimes both. In this case, it would be both, but they still needed to be in alignment. We could take the Presidential Decision Directive, the favorable endorsement from the Office of the Secretary of Defense, and communicate with congressional committees, such as the Armed Services Committees, which oversee defense policy issues. Now we're in the third ring of influence.

We started with the industry, then the agency, and then Congress. We were doing this work together by allowing each of the decision-makers in each of the three rings to understand the technical issues beneath the policy. They want to get the correct answers, but they rely on quality information. This company knew that it could provide the highest quality information to all relevant decision-makers. We were able to help decision-makers communicate with one another faster and more efficiently by assuring that they had relevant information from us and that they could rely on us and trust that what we were telling them was the ground truth. We were the agent that could convey that information.

While we were working on a policy carve out, the clock was ticking for the next legislative session, and the congressional staff found a way to creatively work a specific program carve out that allowed exceptions for a couple of critical programs from being subject to this new desired end state of a law that would reduce our reliance on China. Simultaneously, the company was able to engage in conversations with the Office of the Secretary of Defense, specific to funding that is available through the Defense Production Act, to try to talk about ways that the government could help industry share the cost of bringing the ability to produce this material in the United States back on shore.

That was not in the calculus at the beginning, but it was an opportunity that presented itself as we worked through the challenge. We found a receptive audience that was open to such a partnership.

This magnet material is such that there needs to be a sufficient defense market for a company to make the on-shoring investment decision independently. However, when partnered with the government, it made more economic sense. Eventually that will come to pass; it takes time to achieve that. But, it's a demonstration that we came up with other solutions by working with decision-makers along the way to one solution. We had now simultaneous, positive outcomes in motion.

OUTCOME

Because the company president decided to simultaneously lobby Congress *via* the House Armed Services Committee, the White House Office of Trade Policy, OSD's Office of Industrial Base Policy, the US Navy, and their prime and subprime partners who hire them, the communications generated urgency within the vast bureaucracy and the company achieved the success they needed.

In the next legislative year, Congress passed a law that amended the prior year's law allowing time and space so that industry could work through this challenge with the government to get to a better, good government solution.

Case Study—US Special Operations Command

SITUATION

A small technology company developed an innovative communication system to help Navy SEALs communicate digitally underwater at great distances in extreme conditions. Commercial companies wanted access to the technology, but government rules controlling the dual use of technology jointly developed with the government prohibited such commercial sales.

INTERVENTION

Formulating a unique government engagement plan, the technology company developed a highly effective message and orchestrated a legal and practical exception to the dual-use policy. This carefully crafted message persuaded senior government leaders and decision-makers to approve an exception to policy. This creative workaround allowed the company to adopt a commercially viable alternative that did not require the highest end of military capability.

OUTCOME

This official exception opened up a $100 million-dollar commercial market that would otherwise not have been available.

Case Study—Aircraft Carriers

SITUATION

Aircraft carrier valves and actuators across auxiliary and safety systems were experiencing unacceptably-high failure rates. These systemic failures were directly and negatively impacting fleet readiness by limiting the availability of critical operating and safety systems. The valves' repair costs the US Navy tens of millions of dollars annually, and there was no qualified second source for these critical valves and their actuators. The US Navy would not open a competition to allow others to compete for the work, citing contractual challenges on a contract as large as an aircraft carrier acquisition. They were living in a costly condition.

INTERVENTION

The client understood the operational need and had a better valve product with proven performance that could solve this problem. Bringing the issue, the cost, and the solution to the attention of additional decision-makers would be required. We collaborated to create an integrated, time-sequenced engagement plan with senior government decision-makers. In doing so, we communicated sequentially, and sometimes simultaneously, with the prime contractor, the US Navy aircraft carrier program office, industry trade groups, and finally, congressional defense committees to ensure the challenge and proposed that the solution was both fully recognized.

OUTCOME

The US Navy applied funds to support a competition for a second source, for which the client would be the only competitor. The persistence of our message across the 3-Rings Circus of Federal Sales℠ won the day. Today, this client is displacing the original incumbent valve provider and back fitting valves over time in multiple ships. The long-term impact of this work for the client measures in hundreds of millions of dollars. The return on the investment of time and effort to communicate the problem and solution is nearly incalculable. In the near term alone, the returns exceed 100 times the investment.

Case Study—Safety-at-Sea

SITUATION

The U.S. Navy has used rope "Jacobs" ladders to load sailors and marines from the ship to a small boat and vice versa. Transferring passengers this way is extremely difficult, often requiring a vertical ladder scaling at a distance of over thirty feet. In robust sea states, the evolution is inherently risky. A well-established company in the marine industry understood the problem and had a solution but did not understand how to sell their idea to the federal government.

INTERVENTION

We collaborated on an engagement plan to align the company appropriately with the funding decision-makers. Making the right contacts in the 3-Ring Circus of Federal[SM]: Industry, Agency, and Congress opened new doors of opportunity. The company was provided millions of dollars in funding to demonstrate its expertise with bringing intelligence to metal such that their revolutionary, completely automated, and inherently safer boarding ladder was considered *and funded* for a pilot project.

OUTCOMES

Working with industry, agency, and congressional decision-makers, the company positioned its new offering on the US Navy's newest category of uncrewed surface vessels, opening an entirely new federal funding stream. The future value of this new revenue stream will be in the tens of millions of dollars and sets the stage to apply lessons learned with US Navy customers back into their traditional commercial sales.

Case Study—Let's Build a Ship

SITUATION

Austal USA is a shipbuilder who came to the United States when the US Navy determined they would build the littoral combat ship—LCS. Twenty-plus years ago, the Navy decided, "We're going to change how we do shipbuilding. We want to get faster ships out there. We're going to do it quickly. We're going to break the mold." They allowed the two shipyards (Austal USA and Marinette Marine) to each build a variant of this new type of ship. The Navy would fund shipyards to build ships before the design was complete. (The spidey sense of the engineers reading this goes up.)

This condition was allowed to happen! Congress allowed it to happen, the Navy allowed it to happen, and industry let it happen. It wasn't long before ships were delivering that could not perform. There were high-visibility ship breakdowns, and delays with delivery and repair, and the costs went well above the cost the Navy publicly communicated would make the breakthrough designs worthwhile. The littoral combat ship quickly was labeled the little crappy ship.

Congress was furious this ship was not delivering, it was expensive, and the promises were insincere. Congress threatened to cancel the program. The Navy was pointing fingers at the industry. The industry was pointing fingers at the Navy.

Austal USA, who had come to the United States to do business because they saw that the Navy was going to buy 52 of these ships, now had an existential crisis. Their significant investment may never come to fruition. There were thousands of jobs on the line in Mobile, Alabama and Marinette, Wisconsin, and revenues to suppliers in dozens of states. Were the ship production to stop, this was going to impact not only industry, but also the Navy. These ships were to support a global strategy of presence and deterrence.

INTERVENTION

Austal USA and Marinette Marine had to reset the communications of what was in the public square. Negative headlines, industry articles, and congressional hearing testimony were fraught with inaccuracies. By communicating more clearly the actual facts on the ground, among the 3-Ring Circus of Federal Sales^{SM}, Industry, Agency, and Congress, correct facts could be set on the table so that everybody understood what was really going on. Congress had lousy information. The Navy had incomplete information. Industry didn't have great information. They all got better at it. While they were at it, Austal USA wrung over one million person-days out of the cost of building those ships.

OUTCOMES

Congress reluctantly recognized its role in the poor decisions allowing a program to move too quickly, ahead of the design process. Industry took ownership of its role in allowing itself to move faster than prudent engineering practices of the day would allow. The US Navy was less accountable but would pay a higher price in some ways. The program would be truncated from 52 ships to 32 ships as Navy began to recognize the strategy the ships would support was changing before their eyes.

By stepping back and embracing well-established shipbuilding procedures, both shipbuilders were able to build and deliver a more consistent product that serves the Navy in ways not even intended initially. Today, there are 32 Littoral Combat Ships in the fleet. The Austal USA variant is deployed in the South China Sea and in the Western Pacific, armed with even more powerful deterrent weapons not initially envisioned. The company is now building other types of ships for the US Navy, and the US Coast Guard, including submarine components for the most sensative submarines. The pressures of the challenges set conditions for Austal USA to become highly competitive in aspects of shipbuilding their aluminum shipbuilding roots would not otherwise allow. Austal USA persevered by communicating highly effectively across the 3-Ring Circus of Federal Sales[SM].

Case Study—How DO You Move a Tank?

SITUATION

In the early 2000s, a substantial national security debate surrounded the continuation of building the Abrams M-1 tank. US Army leadership would contend we would not fight another tank war in the future and to continue funding a production line was preventing the Army from spending those dollars on modernization. The logic was appealing to a large part of the national security elite.

However, both industry and Congress understood that if the nation stopped tank production and allowed the line to shut down, industrial capacity would never reemerge or would be incredibly expensive. The manufacturer of the exquisite trailer system required to move a tank to its intended battlefield was in the crossfire of this debate. Tanks don't just drive to their destination; they move on a highly sophisticated trailer system completed with independent articulation for each of several wheels. These trailers are necessary for tank movement.

The tank debate was causing Congress to evaluate whether it could at least temporarily take one billion dollars to fund trailers in the next few years and apply it elsewhere. They would still allow the tank line to stay open but would "mark" the defense appropriations bill to stop funding trailers. This would immediately negatively impact the hundreds of employees who built these trailers in West Plains, Missouri on the steps of the Ozarks where well-paying skill jobs are exceptionally uncommon.

INTERVENTION

The trailer manufacturer recognized their position in the supply chain and the risk to the program. While being a prime contractor of this particular trailer, the utility of the trailer links directly to the funding of the tank it moves. The Army had made its case yet Congress indicated its intent to fund the tank and de-fund the trailer. It is now for industry to underscore additional relevant facts for Congress to consider. Senator Roy Blunt of Missouri was a defense appropriator and a member of the Republican leadership team. The company had three plants in different parts of Missouri, and several hundred employees at each. It doesn't take a rocket scientist to observe that a severe blow to one plant would impact the company's overall performance.

OUTCOME

Communicating relevant facts to the correct decision-maker at the right time and place would cause the "mark" to be reversed by Congress. The trailers would be funded, allowing a one-billion-dollar contract to be booked and assuring the preservation of hundreds of jobs.

Flash forward to 2023, and the war in Ukraine with Russia rages on. Ukraine's President Zelensky desperately pleads with NATO and the United States for tanks to help combat Russia's tanks. Nearly lost in the tank debate of the early 2000s was the United States' Article 5 commitment to NATO; an attack against one is an attack against all. It is sometimes difficult to imagine other theaters of warfare where US equipment may be necessary.

Case Study—You've Got the Wrong Guy!

SITUATION

A provider of video surveillance equipment such as remote cameras and closed-circuit cameras used in security systems throughout the United States was wrongly thought to have Chinese components in their cameras. Congress had identified specific Chinese component providers as expressly prohibited in government-purchased systems. The Department of Defense circulated a poorly-collated listing of companies on what was effectively a "no-buy" list. The equipment company noticed an immediate drop in federal sales and sought to learn why.

INTERVENTION

Communicating concern with their agency customer buying officials, it took little time to learn of the existence of a no-buy list, and that it contained multiple errors. This federal business amounts to nearly $100 million to this company. The company knew it was being unfairly maligned and that buyers were not buying their equipment because they were on this list. We had to work hard to put the correct information in the decision-maker's hands to ensure people knew they had the wrong list. Far up from the buying customer in the Army, Navy, and Air Force, we spoke to senior agency officials in the Office of the Secretary of Defense.

Officials understood our dilemma, but did not want to publicly correct their no-buy list. Left with no option, we spoke to staff members of defense committees in Congress responsible for oversight of DoD. Professional staff understood the business implications, and took interest in how the list came about. DoD officials were asked to detail the process of the list's production.

OUTCOME

After reviewing the sloppy process through which the list was developed DoD, Congress would signal its desire for the list to be corrected. It took a year and a half to do that, but recognizing the leverage and pressure points in the vast department simplified the task. The list was corrected and the federal business soon began to flow again.

Case Study—Seven Dudes and a Good Idea

SITUATION

Beast Code is a small software company in Fort Walton Beach, Florida. The company makes digital visualization tools. Their solutions emanate from gaming technology adapted to demonstrate translation of two-dimensional information into 3D models. The moving models display on tablets for training, documentation, and maintenance support.

The Navy was on the cusp of delivering a revolutionary new class of ship, DDG-1000, and did not have a reliable method of training the sailors to operate the new ship's complex engineering systems. The company came forward on short-notice to deliver a transformational training methodology at a much lower price than classroom "bricks and mortar" training. Sailors could train on their ship with a vast resource of documentation, drawings, and models available in the palm of their hand.

Companies with new technology always struggle to overcome the proverbial "valley of death" between government seed funding and full inclusion in the budget in a program of record. Many companies can't hang on long enough waiting for the budget process to include their new capability. Beast Code's situation could potentially have been such a case, waiting years to be adopted in programs of record that fund other ships (Figure 11.2).

INTERVENTION

Recognizing this capability could easily translate to other classes of ships and even aircraft, Beast Code understood it might be years before this new tool could appear in the Navy budget. By demonstrating its success in the DDG-1000 program, its immediate readiness to adapt to other platforms, and its dramatically cost reduction from the status quo, Beast Code captured the interest of decision-makers across the Navy and in congressional defense committees. Funds were positioned by Congress across multiple programs to support demonstration of this revolutionary capability on several classes of ships, from aircraft carriers to submarines!

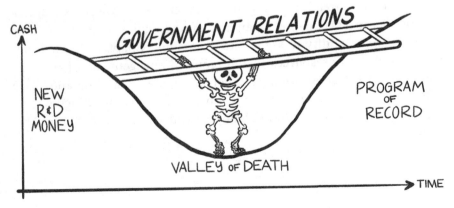

FIGURE 11.2
Traversing the valley of death must be done quickly, and often requires help.

SOLUTION

Because Beast Code's CEO was willing to share their technology openly, and did not cling dearly to their intellectual property, doors were opened across DoD to fund multiple programs with Beast Code's technology. Keys to success include solving an immediate need first (DDG-1000), communicating effectively at the right place and time (Navy and Congress) to demonstrate the product, and not trying to wring every last dollar out of each individual sale. Today, less than ten years later, Beast Code employs over 160 people and its products are in use across every class of US Navy ship. The company's market cap is in the tens of millions and they routinely entertain and dismiss acquisition offers while they continue to grow.

SUMMARY

Chapter 11 demonstrates diverse scenarios of companies addressing vastly different challenges in order to close federal sales. Each of the case studies above is real. Each could resolve in a number of ways, any of which may also be a right answer. Balancing the best outcomes of one's company with the desired and required outcomes of the federal customer is always challenging. The tensions that can emerge among the 3-Rings of Federal Sales^{SM} are completely natural, and an intentional aspect of our system of government.

The common threads running through each case above are the awareness of the process (Chapter 3), an understanding of where lobbying fits (Chapter 2), an ability to see a better outcome (Chapter 4), a willingness to invest the resources in the required engagement (Chapter 5), and a persistent application of expertise at the right time and place (Chapter 6). It nearly goes without saying; doing these things within the prescribed law and policy of lobbying and acquisition (Chapter 7) is always in good form.

Epilogue: Business Tips for Any Executive

There are aspects of federal sales that are unique to every company, product, service and end-customer. Along the spectrum of my work in an agency, in Congress, and in industry as first a corporate lobbyist, and for the past ten years an independent advisor, lobbyist, and consultant, I've picked up on countless tips. There are many more in my repertoire, and you likely have different tips in yours. I have thousands I could share, but this epilogue should stimulate your own creativity and reflection on your work. I share these tips for your consideration in no specific order.

Amp Up Your Wardrobe. You can probably do better. Are you wearing business clothing merely to conform, or is it a true reflection of you? There is room for some creativity, within limits. Stay current, but not trendy. You want to stand out as a professional, not a fashion icon.

Attend Executive-level Seminars and Retreats. Don't wait for your company to foot the bill. Understand that your investment in your professional growth is mostly on you. Attending high-caliber events with leaders and attendees who are achieving higher levels of success will lift you. Doing so will teach you things you presently may not even consider as within your reach. Stretch yourself.

Figure out Who Represents You in Congress. It is completely knowable, and within your grasp to know who your representative and Senators are. You might know them; do they know you? Who in Congress has specific oversight of issues that matter to your company and your customer? Know those people and follow their work, writings, and public comments.

Investing and Taxes. Learn the difference between financial planning and investing. They are not the same, and each has different tax implications. Get professional help. Stop doing your own taxes; it is costing you far more money than a tax professional will save you.

Leadership Training. When speaking to veterans, I emphasize our teaching of leadership tends to focus on positional leadership, lines of authority, and lines of accountability. While those are incredibly important it's not necessarily how the corporate world looks at leadership and it's not necessarily a complete picture. I find that when talking to business leaders about business, the best are able to move the conversation around to include strategic purpose.

Learn when to ask why, as opposed to how. Such distinctions can help open people up and get them to think differently about what it is that they're working on, what they're trying to accomplish, and why they're trying to accomplish it. These are aspects of leadership applied in a strategic sense. My ability to provoke strategic level discussions helps my business and I know it can help you in your corporate setting.

Self-edits. You might be self-editing what's possible because you're looking at work situations through an organizational lens. Who challenges your thinking or the thinking that goes on in your work setting? Are you constrained by organizational parameters? If you're working in a corporation the odds overwhelmingly suggest that you're living within constraints that actually hold you and your company back.

Know Your Value Proposition. Why should the government buy your product or service? What will it do for them? In my case, my value proposition is the expertise I bring to the table, allowing a company to speed through the federal process. Revenues are accelerated by 12–18 months and the ROI of our work typically exceeds 50%–100%. Can you describe your value in one or two sentences?

Control Your Growth. I witness too many companies over-extending themselves based on the promise of future sales because they were awarded a contract with a high "ceiling." Cash is king. Until the sales are put on that high-dollar-value contract, the funds are not available. A booking is not revenue, it's a promise of a future sale—not the same as cash.

Process. I describe myself as a process lobbyist. I am expert at the process, and don't rely on special relationships to carry the day. Success in federal sales requires you to develop expertise in process, and to align your company processes to the federal budget, legislation, acquisition, and contracting processes.

Meetings. Fewer is better, but none is not practical. Why do you block 30 minutes on your calendar for what could and should be a 5- or 10-minute meeting? Likely because that's what your day planner or scheduling software allows. You can mine your calendar for wasted time in nearly every meeting block. Try these tricks: state the purpose and desired outcome of every meeting up front; not everyone needs to speak; forbid the use of "to your point," as it only repeats an accepted solution. I could go on. Put discipline in your meeting regimen.

Write for Public Consumption. Strive to be a thought leader while you are ascending the ladder. Waiting until you promote to a C-Suite position is not the time to learn how to communicate across multiple forms of media. We live in a world of fast-moving information. Don't simply pass others' work around with your comment. Create and publish new and relevant thoughts in your industry. People will notice and follow you—not social media following, real following!

Don't Grow Too Fast. Growth is great, and something all businesses must strive for. If you are not growing, you are on a plateau or are dying. However, you must grow at a rate you can manage. Balancing cash, talent acquisition, production, work flow, supply chains, and more all take thoughtful planning and execution. Don't be the company that outgrows its cash or talent.

Embrace Process. Innovation and revolutionary ideas are not only exciting, they are vital to business growth. You must also establish and adhere to process along the way. There comes a time when the spans of control of leadership become stressed and the leaders can no longer intervene to save the day before something fails. Processes can help you onboard new talent such that they learn and understand what and how the company does what it does.

Know Your Buyer's Journey. This sounds so simple, yet companies often fail to put themselves in their buyer's shoes. What are the next steps in the relationship? What should the buyer expect? When should they expect it, and at what cost? This takes conscious thought to step outside of the day-to-day to immerse in the experience of the buyer's journey. Do you have a secret shopper who does this for you?

Understand Leverage. Sometimes you have leverage with your hands on the lever. Other times you may be someone else's fulcrum, and that lever hurts! Throughout federal sales, there are points of leverage where advantage can be found.

Time. Washington, DC, is run by clocks and calendars. Of course, there are always deadlines, fiscal cliffs, and threats of shutdown to heighten one's awareness of time. Understanding what drives the timelines of federal decisions can offer you leverage and competitive advantage when you apply that understanding.

Sales Navigator on LinkedIn. There once was a time that LinkedIn was where people who hated their jobs secretly made known they were looking. Those days are gone and LinkedIn is the most successful business software tool of our time—because it gets you connected to people. If you don't use the Sales Navigator functions because "my company won't pay for that," you are drowning. I just threw you a life ring. As my brother, a former coast guardsman, says, "I'm going to need you to participate in your own rescue."

Master Classes. Participating in group learning facilitated by experts can help you grow business and interpersonal skills at a very rapid rate. Not all classes are alike and not all cost a lot of money. Your growth will occur only through a bit of vulnerability and discomfort—both are found in Master Classes.

Measure. There are many business books promoting the concept of measuring in business. What you measure, and then what you do with the measurement, is entirely up to you. I won't prescribe any one method of obtaining relevant measures, but if you are not measuring business information, you are losing.

The GI Bill. If you are a veteran, you owe it to yourself to make absolutely sure you understand your benefits. You earned those benefits through uncommon service that only a fraction of the population qualifies for and performs. I nearly missed out because I accepted incorrect information at my time of transition from active duty. By stroke of luck, I was able to fund my Ph.D through veteran's benefit. If you served and want to further your education, make sure you understand your GI Bill benefit.

Trade Show Attendance. Don't be the social coordinator who arranges dinners and golf outings with your posse as you move from show to show. Instead, streamline your trade show attendance to the bare minimum necessary. Approach each show with a specific plan to achieve measurable objectives. Too many migrate with the herd and move from show to show, remaining busy while producing sub-optimal results.

Funding Mechanisms. Learn how money moves in and out of your company. No matter your role, you should understand the process to get your product on contract, and to receive payment from customers. Similarly, take time to understand how your suppliers get paid. How long must they wait for their check? 30, 60, 90 days, or more? If the government is your customer, make sure you know how they pay and exactly when and where their payments will arrive. Knowing these processes can make you a hero in someone's eyes.

Drop the Jargon. Every industry uses its own lexicon replete with buzz-words and acronyms. The defense industry is among the worst offenders. Rather than speak in a language only understood by the military service in which you once served, speak as though communicating with a high school student interested in working in your field. Your words will be more colorful and you'll convey more energy. Everyone knows you're an expert—you don't need to impress anyone with your use of buzzwords and acronyms.

Value. This can be a tricky word for some, but one that must be mastered. Your value to your company and your customer must be known. But first, you must embrace your value by knowing it and demanding others recognize it. Too often, employees sit frustrated because they fail to convey their own value. Your company also has value to a community, to a program, within industry, and perhaps to national security. It's for you to ensure others appreciate your company's value.

Expand Your Personal Choices. When is the last time you tried a new food, wore a new color, attended a different sort of artistic performance, or even tried a new route to drive to work? Humans are creatures of habit. Over time, the habit calcifies into a rut. Don't let it happen to you. We live in a land of opportunity and choice.

Learn How to Use Humor. Humor can humanize any interaction, wrongdoing, or mistake. Self-deprecating humor will always carry the day. When you find yourself in a tense moment, reach for humor rather than the stick.

Social Media. Your buyers are checking you out before you ever walk in the door. What will they already know about you just from your digital footprint?

Preparation. Another lesson in balance. Being prepared to the point that you can't leave your script is a scary place to live. Get comfortable with a degree of ambiguity and you'll learn how to feel comfortable in virtually any setting. You have to know your stuff going into a meeting, but cramming for it isn't the way to go. Successful preparation is taken in daily spoonsful of information, knowledge, dialog, and reflection.

Professional Dress. Conformance may be expected, to a degree. Geographic areas and industries certainly convey an unspoken code of business dress. Is your wardrobe keeping up with the times? There is a balance between fitting in, trying too hard, or just plain standing out. If you are unclear about the balance between appropriate and standing out favorably, don't hesitate to get a professional consultation. Impressions do matter.

Relative Motion. Business and the federal buying process move perpetually. There are no time outs to reset and adjust. Instead, we must adapt to conditions like the political environment, changes of administration, rotation of decision-makers, fiscal calendars, and supply chain challenges. Dealing with conditions in relative motion involves dealing comfortably with a degree of ambiguity. Don't fight it; learn to move with it. Fluid engineers sometimes call this "flow."

Getting Things Done. To accomplish a lot, you must undertake more than might feel comfortable. The key to accomplishment is scheduling an appropriate amount of time for a task. Don't allow tasks to fill the time allotted. Instead of running your day from lists, block time on your calendar. You may have a short list to initially capture ideas, but those must transfer to the action steps of a time and place they will be done. If tasks are on your calendar and you don't complete them as scheduled, move them until complete. You can only move them once or twice. Don't spend more than 30 minutes on any one task unless you really feel the motivation. Knowing you can stop at 30 minutes makes that task easier to start.

Preparation. When giving a presentation, talk, or speech where you will not be reading from a script, you must prepare no matter how good you think you are. The best communicators are not riffing off the cuff, although they might appear to be doing so. Preparation does not necessarily mean devoting a lot of time. It does mean that you need to have worked through the flow, timing, and transitions. When you make this relatively simple act of preparation a habit, you will naturally become, and appear to others, to be a naturally confident presenter. Leadership requires that you confidently communicate in all forms of communication.

Fitness. You don't have to run marathons, triathlons or any extreme races. The realities of aging will creep in. The only way to prolong your physical vitality and stamina is through diet and exercise. I know that's not a news flash. As I look at most people who leave the military quite fit in their early 40s, myself included, gaining 20 pounds in ten years is easy to do. It's not all about the poor choices; your body changes as well. Stay active.

Coalitions Work. When trying to change big policies, don't go it alone. Working together with an association or coalition of associations can make a big difference. There are times where it makes perfect sense to work alongside a competitor in order to achieve a greater good. With correct policies in place, then is the time to proceed with healthy competition.

Be Expert, Not Just Experienced. Being expert is more than just having done something for a long time. Experience suggests you learned something along the way, in part because you understand how to reflect on what you've done or what has happened. Expertise suggests you know how to do something at a very high level and are capable of teaching others through deliberate training or through your actions. Given the choice, strive to be expert.

Change Your Routine. How much sleep did you get last night? Are you in the same pattern of going to bed and waking up at the same time? Do you commute via the same route to work every day? Do you vacation in the same place each year? Do you watch the same programs or read from the same news source every day? How many books did you read or listen to last year? More or less than the year prior? Ask yourself honestly, are you boring? Changing your routine can heighten your interests, and peoples' interest in you!

How Many Beds Will You Sleep in This Year? There is no award for being a road warrior. Don't be proud of how many days you spend on work travel. It may be exciting, to a degree, but will also wear you and your relationships down over time. Travel with intention. Your bed count to revenue ratio might not be an impressive statistic.

End of Year Funds. Any enterprise that operates on a budget offers opportunities for you to seek a redistribution of funds to support that enterprise buying your product or service. Budgets are tools. At the federal level they begin as political documents and then transform into contracting opportunities. In the commercial world, budgets allow a sense of order. In either case, budget allocations are just that, allocations. They are not cast in stone. When opportunities arise to redistribute funds, or capture unobligated funds that didn't spend as planned, be ready!

Embrace Disruption. It drives me nuts to hear someone describe their company as disruptive. To me, that's like an individual calling themselves a genius. Those designations are for others to apply to you. However, the idea of disrupting is positive and should be embraced. Disruption is innovation. Disruption causes discomfort. Growth requires discomfort.

Learn Like Shaq. Over 60% of professional athletes are financially broke within a few years of leaving their professional sport. Shaquille O'Neal is far from broke and is a very savvy business person. Why? Because a close family friend shared critical information with him at the outset of his career. Stated simply, money in a contract is not cash in your hand. The sooner you recognize what part of your earned income is spendable, the richer you will be.

The Best Companies to Work For? Don't chase lists of best companies when seeking a better employment opportunity. Year after year, the big names rise in interest, then quickly fall from favor. Why? Because the lists are based on inconsistent metrics and often rely on the company's telling of its own story. Differentiate favorable press from work culture and company ethics.

How's Your Vision? Too many companies confuse a slogan with a vision statement. Does your company describe its vision with a few words? Fewer than 25? Fewer than 10? Less is more with a vision statement. Don't waste time at corporate off-sites asking for inputs of the 100 top executives. The leadership team should be able to clearly convey corporate vision in 10 words or less.

Credibility. Do what you say you will do. I am routinely amazed by how otherwise talented and competent people let go of credibility by failing to do what they say they will do.

Be Committed. I learned this lesson early from a sage ship Captain. He said, "the chicken is involved in breakfast, but the pig is committed." There's a difference. One can only die on their sword once, and I'm not suggesting that option. But commitment requires much more than merely being involved. I saw a guitar duo playing in the Nashville airport to an empty restaurant at 7:30 am. Are you that committed to your craft or your work?

Don't Be a Lobster. Some know that lobsters swim by fiercely swatting their tail to propel them backward. One quick thrust will move the lobster a considerable distance. Don't be seen at work as a lobster who backs away from challenges or problems.

Keep Your Messaging Fresh. We've all seen bananas that get a little too ripe. Some prefer the sweetness of a slightly overripe banana. But there comes a time when it's just distasteful. Don't let your messaging get too dated.

When You Tell the Truth, You Become a Resource. Being known as someone who is knowledgeable in your industry and company, who is also willing to tell the truth without spin, will differentiate you. When company leaders or industry and congressional decision-makers respect your inputs, you are now a resource. Truth-telling is an essential ingredient of your identification as a resource.

Essential Briefing Tips. 1. Respect your audience's time. 2. Don't tell them everything you know. 3. Identify your proposal's benefits. 4. Identify the corollary to your proposal's benefits.

Your First Answer Might be Right. In the discovery of longitude, the chronometer was "good enough" nearly 50 years before it was accepted as a solution to the long-held pursuit to understand this critical component of long-distance navigation at sea. Think of the Pareto principle (the 80/20 rule). Eighty percent is likely good enough for nearly any solution. Move out and correct the rest as you go.

Conditions Change Quickly. The pandemic was not predicted, yet took hold globally and quickly. Recessions result largely from psychological responses to perceived changes of conditions. International conflicts can occur over a weekend, and change global dynamics in fuel prices, travel options, and migrations of people. When I deployed in Navy ships, I came to recognize that six months is a long time and some sort of global event will likely happen over the course of those six months. How imaginative are you in your preparation for uncertain events?

Index

Note: *Italic* page numbers refer to figures.

Printed in the United States
by Baker & Taylor Publisher Services